# The Place of the Classroom
# and the Space of the Screen

new
literacies
q

AND DIGITAL EPISTEMOLOGIES

Colin Lankshear and Michele Knobel
*General Editors*

Vol 50

The New Literacies and Digital Epistemologies series
is part of the Peter Lang Education list.
Every volume is peer reviewed and meets
the highest quality standards for content and production.

PETER LANG
New York • Washington, D.C./Baltimore • Bern
Frankfurt • Berlin • Brussels • Vienna • Oxford

NORM FRIESEN

# The Place of the Classroom
# and the Space of the Screen

Relational Pedagogy and Internet Technology

PETER LANG
New York • Washington, D.C./Baltimore • Bern
Frankfurt • Berlin • Brussels • Vienna • Oxford

Library of Congress Cataloging-in-Publication Data

Friesen, Norm.
The place of the classroom and the space of the screen:
relational pedagogy and internet technology / Norm Friesen.
p. cm. — (New literacies and digital epistemologies; v. 50)
Includes bibliographical references and index.
1. Distance education—Computer-assisted instruction.
2. Education—Effect of technological innovations on.
3. Educational technology. I. Title.
LC5803.C65F75    371.35'8—DC22    2010026821
ISBN 978-1-4331-0959-1 (hardcover)
ISBN 978-1-4331-0958-4 (paperback)
ISSN 1523-9543

Bibliographic information published by **Die Deutsche Nationalbibliothek**.
**Die Deutsche Nationalbibliothek** lists this publication in the "Deutsche
Nationalbibliografie"; detailed bibliographic data is available
on the Internet at http://dnb.d-nb.de/.

FSC
**Mixed Sources**
Product group from well-managed
forests, controlled sources and
recycled wood or fiber
Cert no. SCS-COC-002464
www.fsc.org
©1996 Forest Stewardship Council

Cover and interior design by Mauve Pagé

The paper in this book meets the guidelines for permanence and durability
of the Committee on Production Guidelines for Book Longevity
of the Council of Library Resources.

*To the memory of my mother and my father*
*—teachers both.*

# Contents

# *Preface*

HAVING BEEN INVOLVED IN WEB-BASED EDUCATION FROM ITS start in the mid-1990s, I have seen many trends come and go. From dotcom-era startups, e.g., Cardean, UNext, Fathom, to learning objects, or from laptop universities to Web 2.0, there has been no shortage of buzzwords, predictions, and promises. With all these apparent changes, though, some elements of online learning have been remarkably stable: Student interaction and communication have remained a central concern—from bulletin boards to Twitter—and the wealth of resources available online—from Java Applets to Podcasts—has consistently held out an elusive promise. One further persistent element in online learning is perhaps less prominent or obvious than these two examples, and it takes the form of a question. Indeed, this question is raised repeatedly with remarkable consistency and insistency, across a wide range of settings and contexts. It is a question that has been asked, in different ways, in casual conversations, in more formal discussions for institutional planning and support, as well as in academic publications in educational technology and distance education. The question is about the differences between online and offline education—between classroom and screen—and the significance of these differences for teaching and learning.

It is not uncommon to hear students making observations such as, "I like the flexibility of online courses," or "I miss the spontaneity of learning face-to-face." Teachers may sometimes observe, for example, that "online, quiet students are able to open up and be more vocal," or that "in the classroom, you can see and respond to the students' nodding heads or glazed eyes." Texts providing guidelines for online teachers warn of the differences separating Web and classroom, saying for example, that "because face-to-face contact is not available, it is good practice to respond as quickly as possible" to online student queries (DBU, 2007). Innumerable research papers have explored the implications of these kinds of observations and comments in more formal terms, using a range of strategies for investigation and argumentation. For example, many researchers have rigorously compared "online students" with "lecture students" (Dutton, Durron & Perry., 2002), or class "communication…online and face-to-face" (Weaver et al., 2009) or "student success in face-to-face and distance teleclass environments" (Deka & McMurray, 2006).

The question of the differences between online and face-to-face situations for teaching and learning can be said to form a figurative "red thread" that is woven into the fabric of both formal and informal discussions of online education. This thread can be traced as far back as some of the earliest texts on the use of the Internet in education, and it follows a path into the present where it can be identified in discussions, for example, of Web 2.0 in teaching and learning. This insistent question remains, even as trends come and go, and as practical and technical issues—like increased campus bandwidth or course development strategies—are first raised and then addressed. When this "red thread" is tugged on or teased out, it has the effect of loosening others, of disrupting the way that the discourse of online education is conventionally woven together or articulated. In this book, by tugging at and following this thread, some of the fabric that constitutes common understandings of online teaching and learning is unraveled. The question of the difference between online and offline contexts for education is one that ties together many aspects of what it means to teach and to study, both online and offline.

It is clear that this red thread has woven its way through many different discursive folds and patterns over time. The question of the differences between online and offline has been addressed in different ways in various kinds of discussions and debates since the advent of the Internet as a popular medium. One early debate is of particular importance for the difference between online and offline teaching. Therefore, it is referenced and discussed at a number of points in this book, with an overview provided here. This debate is concerned first of all with what could be called a "transmission model" of communication, and with a more general and related "technologized" view of teaching, learning, and experience.

## The Transmission Model of Communication

Around the turn of the century, at a time when online and offline were conceptualized in relatively simple, black-and-white terms, the "virtual" and the "real" were envisioned as two discrete and mutually opposed realms. Their differences were highlighted in bold and optimistic proclamations of the independence of the virtual from the physical. The 1996 "Declaration of the Independence of Cyberspace," for example, asserts that:

> Our world is different. Cyberspace consists of transactions, relationships, and thought itself, arrayed like a standing wave in the web of our communications. Ours is a world that is both everywhere and nowhere, but it is not where bodies live. We are creating a world that all may enter without privilege or prejudice accorded by race, economic power, military force, or station of birth. (Barlow, 1996)

During these early days, the Internet was thought of as a network of "collective intelligence" (Levy, 1997) or a "civilization of the mind" (Barlow, 1996), which was seen as separate from and even self-sufficient vis-à-vis the physical world "where our bodies live."

On one side of the debate are arguments for the freedom and convenience opened up by the online world, and on the other side are claims concerning the authenticity or the familiar tangibility of face-to-face engagement offline. For example, in *The Virtual Community* (2000), Harold Rheingold enthusiastically describes how he and others in the San Francisco area were able to "find communion in cyberspace" by connecting together with modems and early bulletin board technologies (p. 8). On the other side of the debate, Hubert Dreyfus's *On the Internet* (2001) gives pride of place to the phenomenon of *embodiment* in learning. Dreyfus argues that, although learners may be able to achieve a kind of rote-level "competency" online, they will never be able to attain professional "mastery" because the "Net's limitations where embodiment [and] face-to-face learning... [are]

concerned... may well leave students stuck [just] at competence" (p. 39). The intuitive and practiced understanding that Dreyfus associates with higher levels of learning apparently forever remains beyond the reach of the online learner.

Dreyfus's arguments initially stirred up considerable controversy (e.g., Tripathi, 2002; Land, 2005) and his book continues to attract interest—as a recent revision and reissue of *On the Internet* (2008) attests. One early rebuttal of Dreyfus's position was provided by Stephen Downes (2002), a renowned commentator on online learning. Downes bases his counter-argument on the assumption that the Web and the Internet, like books and films, provide viewers or users with a kind of indirect or "mediated" experience of the world. However, Downes goes further: Every kind of experience, he contends, is mediated in some way—whether by words, digital information, or by physical processes of perception. "All experience is, to a degree, mediated, either through the waves of light and sound that interact with our senses, or even through the nerve impulses that carry the impact of a physical event in our toes to our brain" (2002). Downes then reasons that the kind of vicarious or "mediated experience" provided to us through film, fiction, and the Internet can be just as real, authentic, and educationally valuable as the immediate embodied experience that Dreyfus privileges:

> It seems to me that Dreyfus overlooks entirely the possibility that the mind can engage, through intermediate sources, the reality that lies at the other end of the interface. Indeed, it should be remarked that this is a natural and normal function of the mind, and that this is something that we must do every instant of our lives. All experience is... [after all] mediated... (2002, n. p.)

The claim that "all experience is mediated" is key. It encapsulates a way of understanding experience that is diametrically opposed experience and experiential meaning as they are affirmed in this book. Viewing experience a kind of collection of "data" is of paramount importance to Downes's critique, and has also been central in the Western philosophical tradition, from Ancient Greece through the Enlightenment, to present-day cognitive science. According to this understanding, every sort of experience, whether "im-mediate," simulated or vicarious, is part of a "constant flow of sensory input" that, as Downes explains, we are "at all times amassing and assessing." All experience, in this view, can be reduced to a question of receiving sensory material, information, or data. This experiential information, in turn, provides the mind with "the materials" for its "reason and knowledge" (Locke, 1690, n.p.). This particular way of defining "experience" and "knowledge" has traditionally been associated with the philosophy of *empiricism.* According to this philosophy, the precise origin of experiential data before they are received and processed by the mind is relatively unimportant. Whether these data are transmitted digitally and then presented on a screen, or communicated more "directly" via soundwaves or nerve impulses is unimportant. In the end, as Downes emphasizes, the Internet and the Web are "a channel for information about the world, no more or no less than any other channel: like a book, like a movie, like our direct perception of the world around us" (2002, n. p.). In this text, I argue that books, movies, and other media can provide for very powerful experiences, but I also maintain that this type of experience is clearly different from "direct perception of the world around us."

Many texts on online education written both before and after this debate repeat Downes's basic argument. In both general and educational contexts, it is easy to find a vocabulary of "data" and "signals" being used to describe what is occurring in human communication, both online and off. Studies of computer mediated communication, for example, have long spoken of "signals" or "cues" being either faithfully transmitted (as in face-to-face and high-tech video conferencing contexts) or as being "filtered out" (in communications that involve just voice or textual transmission). While state-of-the-art videoconferencing technologies are said to retain as many cues and data as possible, voice communications are seen as necessarily filtering out cues that are visual in nature. Text-based communications (letters, emails, online chats) correspondingly filter out a much wider range of data. Of course, the assumption behind this approach—often referred to as the "cues filtered-out model"—is that communication is ultimately about sending and receiving cues, signals, or data. According to this approach, in contrast to my own rather different understanding, technology is paramount. The more faithfully and comprehensively that a given technology can transmit data—such as tone of voice, pauses, and facial expression—the "richer" the communication is. And the less a given technology transmits, the "poorer" or "leaner" it is:

> oral interaction in a face-to-face context provides multiple non-verbal or paralinguistic cues such as facial expression and tone of voice. Socially and emotionally, face-to-face oral interaction is a rich medium. In contrast, text-based interaction might be termed a lean medium, in that much of the information that creates and sustains the group dynamic of face-to-face groups is simply not transmitted. (Lu et al., 2007, p. 4412; see also Garrison, Anderson, & Archer, 2000, p. 90)

Communication, in this line of thinking, is thus a question of transmitting and receiving signals, cues, or information, either in greater or lesser amounts. Ultimately, the question of effective communication ends up with a rather predictable answer: communication becomes more effective with more and better technology. The issue of communication, in other words, is "technologized." Superior audio and video transmission and connectivity with greater capacity will result in fewer "cues" and signals being filtered out, resulting in a superior context for communication. To take this view further, one area of interdisciplinary research drawing from psychology and electronic and acoustical engineering has focused on the challenges of improving and refining transmission and reproduction in the name of "presence" or "immediacy." The idea that communication and even presence are principally a matter of transmitting information reaches from various fields of research to commonsense talking and thinking. Linguists and psychologists, for example, have long pointed out how common phrases like "it's hard to get that idea across," or "his words carry little meaning" underscore the notion of "communication as transmission" (Lakoff & Johnson, 1980).

## Moving Beyond a Technologized View of Experience, Learning, and Teaching

These kinds of metaphors and language of a "technologized" understanding of communication, experience, and education are one of the principal impediments, however, to comprehending the differences between online and offline experience. If experience is ultimately seen as a question of receiving and transmitting information or sense data, then many subtle differences that separate the physical classroom from the computer screen are rendered relatively arbitrary and unimportant. Given the right conditions, data and information, according to this argument, can be sent and received very effectively in both contexts.

If there were nothing more to communication—or to experience—than the undifferentiated transmission of information through nerve impulses or Internet bandwidth, this book would be short indeed. If the difference between online and offline education were limited to the quantities and types of data and information, such differences could be readily comprehended and counteracted with greater bandwidth and better technology. As this book shows, however, questions of communication, experience, and also of "presence" are not that simple. The vocabulary of "data," "information," "channels," and "transmission" may make sense when talking about the operations of computers and the Internet, but their usefulness is rather limited when discussing the value of these same technologies specifically for *education*. For education, online and offline need to be discussed in a language sensitive to human experience and attentive to questions of meaning and significance, rather than in a vocabulary based on computational operation. A language sensitive to human expression and meaning allows persons to say they feel "distant" from someone who is physically next to them, or "close" to someone who is far away, when that individual's "presence" is only manifest as words on a screen or letters on a page. What is needed is a vocabulary and set of criteria, in which a technology or medium is not judged in terms of its informational richness or poverty, but in terms of its *experiential* qualities—in terms of *felt* immediacy or distance, for example. This kind of language and frame of reference, moreover, are not intrinsically opposed to or critical of technology, but they emphatically do *not* describe or judge technology on its own instrumental or "technical" terms. Instead, it is more explicitly grounded in or attuned to the human ends that technology is ultimately supposed to serve. As the concluding chapters of this book will show, recognizing and sustaining this vocabulary and way of thinking in the face of relentless instrumentalization in education are a primary challenge for both educational research and practice.

# Acknowledgments

FOR A PROJECT ENCOMPASSING A DECADE, IT IS NOT SUR-prising that an author has many specific contributions to acknowledge and many individuals to thank. First, I owe a considerable debt of gratitude to my *Doktorvater*, Max van Manen, who very patiently and supportively oversaw the development of this text at a very early stage in the form of my doctoral dissertation. Max's help and influence were invaluable not only for guiding me through the myriad tasks and possibilities of phenomenological research, but also for re-awakening my interest in German and continental under-standings of *Bildung* and pedagogy as expressions of cultural practice. This interest was developed further through my association with Tone Saevi, of the Norwegian Teachers' Academy in Bergen. During her extended teach-ing and research visit to Thompson Rivers University in Kamloops, Tone led a class of student teachers through some of the aspects of relational pedagogy that are central to this book. In both her articulation and prac-tice of pedagogy, Tone had a significant influence on my engagement with these issues and on the treatment of these topics in this book. I also owe a debt of gratitude to Eetu Pikkarainen and his colleagues for a produc-tive visit to the University of Oulu in 2009. During their stay, I was able to give presentations on a number of topics central to this text. Stephan Hopmann of the University of Vienna, David Seamon of Kansas State University, Bernard Irrgang of the Technical University of Dresden, Robert Rosenberg of the Georgia Institute of Technology, and Andrew Feenberg of Simon Fraser University are all deserving of my gratitude for their ideas and encouragement at specific points in this book's development. The outstanding assistance of Merilee Hamelock for bibliographic and proofing tasks and of Johanne Provençal for organizational strategies and emphasis for this publication also deserves special notice.

Thanks are also due to a number of organizations whose assistance has been critical in making this book possible: the support of the Social Sciences and Humanities Research Council of Canada (in the form of a Postdoctoral Fellowship and Standard Research Grant), the Infrastructure Fund of the Canada Foundation for Innovation, and the Canada Research Chair Program.

Finally, I owe a much greater debt of gratitude to those who "lived" through the experience of writing this book with me. For the unfailing support and patience of my wife, Barbara Simler, I am indebted beyond all repayment.

Some of the material has been previously published. Much of chapter five appears in an article, "Dissection and Simulation: Brilliance and Transparency, or Encumbrance and Disruption?" that forms the basis for a special section in *Techne: Research in Philosophy and Technology*. A very short version of chapter five is also available in the newsletter *Environmental & Architectural Phenomenology*. Parts of chapters six and seven in the present text appear as a chapter titled "Pedagogy in the Classroom and on the Screen: A Phenomenological Hermeneutic Analysis" in the book *Erziehung— Phänomenologische Perspektiven*, edited by Malte Brinkmann and published by Könighausen & Neumann. Finally, a very early version of parts of chapters six and seven were published in 2002 as the chapter "Is There a Body in This Class?" which appeared in the collection *Writing in the Dark*, edited by van Manen and published by Althouse Press.

*section one*

SETTING UP THE QUESTION,
QUESTIONING THE SET-UP

# CHAPTER 1

# *Introduction*

*When my answer is wrong, I know it immediately because my teacher, Per, looks at me with this particular humorous glance and says, after just a tiny little pause: "Yes...?" Then I understand that he wants me to give the question a second thought. He just leans back comfortably and waits. That's why I like him so much. I feel relaxed and smart with him.*

    —FROM SAEVI (2005)

*Imagine my surprise when I checked my blog the next day, and saw a comment from someone named Ari in Germany: "Nice story, Janet! I really like the fact that you got some help from others in Canada to get your project page done. I think this is very important in wikis." In the days that followed, Ari's comments boosted my confidence and motivated me to complete my first contribution to* Wikipedia.

    —ADAPTED FROM FRIESEN & HOPKINS (2008)

THE TWO SHORT PASSAGES ABOVE COME FROM TWO RATHER different sources and depict two quite different situations: the first is from a collection of interviews with special needs students in a high school in Norway. The second is from an account of an open online course in which adult students from around the world learned about making contributions to collaborative projects such as *Wikipedia*. Both descriptions focus on a different educational sector—school in one case and adult education in the other. Both involve a different cultural and linguistic context: Norwegian compulsory education and voluntary education in an international setting.

Despite these differences, these two passages share important commonalities. Both are illustrative of a kind of descriptive, almost literary style of writing that reappears at many points in this book and that plays an important role in its reflections on the place of the classroom and the space of the screen. Both also present a common theme of pedagogical significance: the issue of *relationship* in teaching and learning, and the significance of tactfully cultivating an appropriate tone in these relationships. In the first description, it is the teacher's "particular humorous glance," and the kind and patient manner in which he responds to the student's mistaken answer that exemplifies this tone and tact. In the second, it is Ari's positive and enthusiastic comments ("Nice story, Janet!...") that are illustrative of some of these same relational qualities.

There is another factor evident in these two short passages that is also central to this book: the nature of the location in which the exchanges take place. One passage describes a physical classroom while the other depicts events occurring online. This difference is indicated not only by how the second description speaks of the online technologies of blogs and wikis; it is also illustrated in the way in which the relational qualities mentioned above are manifest. In the first, "face-to-face" description, it is the careful *pause* and *glance* of the teacher that is highlighted; in the second, it is the kind, written *words* of "Ari in Germany" that are significant.

There are, of course, many differences that separate "offline" from "online," and "face-to-face" from "cyberspace." As illustrated in the preface, the way in which these differences have been understood has changed over time. In the 1990s, when the Internet came into popular use, these differences were seen as pronounced and in terms that sometimes tended to be rather black and white. However, with the passage of time, hard-and-fast differences between experiences online and offline have diminished. It is important to briefly trace this change and its implications in order to frame the question central to this study. Seeing offline and online simply as two separate worlds, as one sociologist observes, "is far too simple" (Slater, 2002 p. 533). "[T]he binary opposition between cyberspace and 'the real world,'" others have noted, "is not nearly as sharp or clean as it's [been] made out to be" (Kolko, Nakamura,

& Rodman, 2000, p. 4). The gradual blurring of the distinctions between cyberspace and "the real world" is due to a number of factors, one of these being the gradual introduction of online approximations of many activities that earlier took place only face-to-face. Banking, shopping, learning, teaching, and even criminality, to name just a few examples, have now had counterparts online for some time. Moreover, it is significant that in all of these cases, the same words are used to designate what happens both virtually and in "reality": We speak of banking, shopping and learning online, and hear of news reports of "cyber crime."

Similarly, when it comes to schooling and education, specialized and everyday forms of expression have the effect of neutralizing the differences between online and offline experiences. Face-to-face as well as online settings are spoken of as classrooms and seminars where processes of "communication" and "interaction" occur. In this sense, it is possible, for example, to casually "chat" or to hold formal academic "discussions" in a classroom or seminar either online or offline. Similarly, students—both online and offline—are asked to work through various curricular "contents" and are provided by their teachers with appropriate evaluative "feedback." When described and understood in these ways, it is easy to suppose that Internet and computer technologies present a kind of "neutral" ground for human contact in general and for the roles and activities of education in particular.

Alas, it is not so simple. As illustrated in the two passages above, pedagogy involves issues as broad as personal relationships and as subtle as tact and tone. Just because we sometimes use the same language to talk about our activities online and offline does not mean that we confuse "virtual" experiences with those taking place face-to-face. Receiving an email from someone is obviously not the same as getting a phone call. Moreover, both are different from a greeting "in the flesh." We experience "presence" and "proximity" differently in these two settings. At the same time, we are challenged to find the proper descriptive language to draw out these differences in a manner that is both clear and compelling. Still, the differences remain.

*So what exactly are the differences embedded in our educational experiences, online and offline? What are the terms and frames of reference that are suited to knowing and understanding them? Finally, what is their relationship to pedagogy?*

It is these kinds of questions that lie at the heart of this book. Indeed, it is the purpose of this introductory chapter to consider ways in which such questions are best set up or formulated for closer consideration. These questions, like others that are of sustained concern in education, do not have simple answers. In considering them, the context provided by existing research and practice and the way that related questions have been addressed are both important. This introductory chapter consequently undertakes a contexualization of this general domain, focusing on two areas in particular:

1. On similar questions that have been addressed in educational research in the past and that are still being investigated today;
2. On related questions that have been raised and addressed concerning technology more generally.

By considering these two areas, it will be possible to reformulate more precisely the queries posed in italics above—and to condense them into a single, pointed question that will frame and guide the book overall.

## The Difference That Makes a Difference

This book presents a way of questioning the "virtual" and the "real" in education in a manner that departs from similar questioning in the past. In fact, in both educational technology and distance education, there has been *one* dominant way in which these kinds of questions have been posed: in terms of educational efficiency or *outcomes*. Although pedagogy is relevant to a wide range of issues— from those as broad as personal relationships to those as subtle as tact and tone—the emphasis in research is squarely on the outcomes produced by the introduction of technology into pedagogical contexts. Specifically, student performance in a course that uses a technology is compared in these studies to a similar course in which the same technology is absent. It is not surprising that this uniform body of research has produced similarly uniform results. Research comparing the effectiveness of technology-based courses to those taught in the classroom has repeatedly shown that there is "no significant difference" between the two. The regularity with which this finding has been produced has given rise to "the no significant difference phenomenon" (Russell, 1999, 2008). In his book and on his Web site, Russell looks at hundreds of studies conducted over dozens of years, all of which arrive at this same conclusion. From print-based correspondence courses to classes taught via radio, television, and the Web, the use of technologies in each case was *not* found to make a statistically significant difference in instructional outcomes. When compared with students' achievement in more traditional classroom settings, any differences detected by these studies fall within acceptable margins of error or statistical insignificance. As one recent report cited by Russell states, "No significant differences were found between... traditional and distance students in [their] mean scores" (Smith & Palm, 2007, p. 215; as cited in Russell, 2008). Frames of reference provided by outcomes or measures of instructional effectiveness have thus been used in attempts to answer the question of pedagogical differences separating the virtual and the real. This way of framing the question has produced unsatisfactory or at least inconclusive results: online and offline teaching and learning have repeatedly been shown to be equivalent in terms of their educational efficiency, with the conclusion that one is not significantly different from the other. However, as this book shows, in the experiences of teachers and students, online and offline education *are* clearly different; and in light of this fact, we must not continue to ignore these differences. We need different ways of both asking and seeking to answer questions about technology, education, and human experience in order to understand the significant differences between the virtual and the real in education.

In this book, I take up ways of asking and answering questions that are quite different from most research in educational technology and online learning. This difference is reflected in the writing style, in the kind of evidence provided, and in the way that this evidence is interpreted and discussed in the book. These different characteristics should be clear from the way I have opened this introductory chapter, and from the way I develop my central question in the next section. These characteristics can be enumerated as follows: First, as noted earlier, passages that are primarily descriptive or even literary in nature are used in this introduction and throughout this book. They are employed as of a kind of "evidence" for studying experience in online and offline settings. As I explain in the next chapter, this type of evidence is indispensable in coming to an understanding of human experience and its meanings. Second, in discussing experience and its significance,

I use terms and categories that are as close to, rather than far away from, the realm of everyday experience. Consequently, I have written this book in a style that is as accessible as possible, and that avoids unnecessary techno-logical or methodological specialization and complexity. Instead, I rely on terms as simple as the pronouns I, *you*, and *we* as ways of explaining my methods and analytic categories. Third, I devote considerable attention to language itself: to the vocabularies and metaphors that are used to discuss online technology generally and to the specific terminology that I myself use in this study.

## A Human-Scientific Inquiry

Broadly speaking, the three characteristics just described are in keeping with what could be called the human science orientation of this study. The word "science" in this context refers to something quite different from the natural sciences and methods of experimental investigation associated with them. It refers instead to study or scholarship more generally, and is a translation of part of the German term for the human sciences, the *Geisteswissenschaften*—literally, the sciences of the intellect or spirit. One particular approach taken by a number of "scientists" or philosophers in this field goes by the name of *phenomenology*, and focuses on the systematic study of human experience. Edmund Husserl (1859–1938) is widely regarded as the father of phenomenology. Together with successive generations of his students—particularly Martin Heidegger and Hans-Georg Gadamer—he helped pioneer ways of thinking and questioning that are central to this book. Husserl inaugurated a century-long phenomenological tradition by asking questions primarily about *epistemology*, questions concerning how we know about the world around us, both in formal, scientific terms and in the context of everyday experience.

In his *Crisis of the European Sciences* (1936) Husserl characterizes the human sciences as having their origin in concrete "every-day sense experi-ence," in what he refers to as the *lifeworld*, rather than in the realm of scien-tific and mathematical specialization and abstraction. Husserl does not seek to deny the natural sciences and their predictive and explanatory power, however. He attempts instead to understand this power in its relationship to everyday experience and knowledge, and what he calls its "concrete" and "intuitively given" character. Husserl sees everyday ways of knowing as having an integrity and validity of their own, and argues further that this "lifeworld" knowledge actually comes before and is fundamental to specialized scientific knowledge. "Natural-scientific mathematization," according to Husserl, only serves to measure and explain what is always already "there" for us in the world of our everyday experience:

> In ... natural-scientific mathematization, in the open infinity of possible experiences, we measure the life-world—the world constantly given to us as actual in our concrete world-life—for a well-fitting garb of ideas, that of the so-called objectively scientific truths. In this way we obtain possibilities of predicting concrete occurrences in the intuitively given life-world, occurrences which are not yet or no longer actually given. And this kind of prediction infinitely surpasses the accomplishment of everyday prediction. (p. 51)

The abstract scientific world of particles, forces and the causality of their interaction—despite their "well fitting" precision and universality—does not invalidate the integrity and importance possessed by everyday experience, and the life-world in which this experience is located. Although scientific accounts may be capable of covering this reality like a "well-fitting garb," the lifeworld is both independent and rather different from these accounts. Husserl continues:

> Mathematics and mathematical science, as a garb of ideas, or the garb of symbols of the symbolic mathematical theories, encompasses everything which, for scientists and the educated generally, represents the life-world, dresses it up as "objectively actual and true" nature. It is through the garb of ideas that we take for true being what is actually a method. (p. 51; original emphases)

Scientific explanations and calculations, for Husserl and for human science, are valuable as techniques or means for achieving prediction and control. Even so, they are not an ultimate account of what is true or what ultimately "is." Natural science can provide explanations for things we experience, but these mathematically based sciences do not explain them *away*; they do not exhaustively account for the depth and colour of emotions or the intensity and vividness of the senses, for example. Human scientists, as a further example, would disagree with formulations by the natural scientist

Lord Kelvin who once said: "When you can measure what you are speaking about, and express it in numbers, you know something about it; but when you cannot express it in numbers, your knowledge is of a meager and unsatisfactory kind" (quoted in Scheper-Hughes, 1992, p. 202). There are many forms of experiential knowledge that have little if nothing to do with measurement, and there are also many kinds of qualitative differentiation (or improvement) that similarly evade quantification. This separation between experience and measurement is central to this book. It underlies, for example, this book's attempt to understand the difference between online and offline in experiential terms rather than in measurements of student performance.

Martin Heidegger, one of Husserl's students, developed this way of thinking further through an emphasis on *ontology*, on questions of *being* rather than on those of knowledge and *epistemology*. Heidegger follows Husserl's idea that there are different ways of knowing, or rather, of being engaged with the world, specifically those that are more formal and abstract, and those that are more concrete and commonplace. However, in exploring these differences, Heidegger uses a human science vocabulary that is more idiosyncratic and enigmatic than that of his teacher. He also turns his attention not to science and mathematics, but to questions concerning technology, and how technology shapes our "being." Heidegger critiqued the notion that technology (and the scientific principles that it, in part, instantiates) stands on its own and is thus separate from the way we "are" and what we experience. Instead, he insisted that technology frames our experience and understanding in particular ways, and he warned that technology had the potential to frame our world and our being in such as manner as to diminish our openness to the character of our own "being."

Heidegger was also closely attentive to the significance of language in knowing and being, and once said that language itself "speaks" in and through us and that "language is the house" of our being. One of the principle contributions of his student Gadamer is to explain Heidegger's unusual insights in a way that is considerably less figurative and allusive. What Gadamer says about language, however, clearly resonates with Heidegger's images and evocations. Gadamer (2004) argues that words are not simple signs that are to be attached to items or concepts in the world like labels.

"A word is not just a sign," he insists; "language is more than just a sign sys-tem denoting the totality of objects" (p. 416). Instead, Gadamer maintains that language and experience actually arise together, that they literally "co-emerge" (Lye, 1996):

> *Experience is not wordless to begin with, subsequently becoming an object of reflection by being named, by being subsumed under a universality of the word. Rather, experience of itself seeks and finds words that express it. We seek the right word –i.e., the word that really belongs to the thing—so that in it the thing comes into language. (2004, p. 417)*

We do not live in a meaningless world devoid of names and categories that is subsequently given meaning only with the right names and categories. We do not, for example, enter a classroom, and piece together evidence of bodies and furnishings to reach the conclusion that the labels of class, classroom, desks, and students would apply. Our encounter with the class and the room and its meanings (which can, of course, vary widely) instead arise together, simultaneously. They are inextricably interdependent and intertwined. As Gadamer further explains:

> *Language is not just one of man's possessions in the world, but on it depends the fact that man has a world at all. For man the world exists as world in a way that no other being in the world experiences. But this world is linguistic in nature.... That which can be understood is language... language has no independent life apart from the world that comes to language within it. Not only is the world world only insofar as it comes into language, but language, too, has its real being only in the fact that the world is presented in it... (p. 441)*

The world, or more specifically, the life-world, is always already linguistic in nature. Experiencing the world and engaging with language are, in a sense, inseparable.

### Questioning As a Path

Martin Heidegger understood the question as being about much more than matters of fact, truth, and falsehood. He describes "questions" as represent-ing "paths toward an answer" (1992a, p. 431). Heidegger emphasizes that as a figurative path, a question does not lead to an answer that has the form of "a propositional statement about a matter at stake" (1992a, p. 431). Instead, Heidegger explains that "if an answer could be given" to such a question, this answer "would consist in a transformation of thinking" (1992a, p. 431). To paraphrase Heidegger's language, one could say that the path represented by the question does not lead to a final destination. Instead, it holds out the possibility of a change in thinking about matters at hand. Gadamer, again putting Heidegger's expression slightly less figuratively, explains that "The essence of the *question* is to open up possibilities and keep them open" (2004, p. 299; original emphasis). In order to present a path toward an answer, Gadamer suggests that a question should not be framed or articulated in a way that unnecessarily forecloses on certain answers, or that already points to a known or predetermined answer: "the openness of what is in question consists in the fact that the answer is not settled" (2004, p. 363). To reiterate, it is precisely the point of this chapter to formulate or set up this kind of open, "unsettled," and potentially even unsettling question. In his famous essay, "The Question Concerning Technology" (1992b), Heidegger seeks to open up a path of questioning for technology generally. By first briefly turning to Heidegger's own question about technology, this chapter will frame the question that ultimately guides and motivates this book as a whole. In his early work, Heidegger describes technology in terms of a "totality" or "ensemble." Any one piece of technology or equipment, Heidegger explains, necessarily belongs to the "totality of equipment" in which it is used (1962, pp. 97–98). A hammer presupposed the availability of nails; a computer presupposes the existence and interchange of data (e.g., on the Internet). Later, Heidegger came to describe technology and the totality in which it is manifest by using the German word "*Gestell*" (1992b). This term has been translated variously as an "enframing," "installation," "emplacement" or even as a "set-up." As Samuel Weber (1989) describes it, Heidegger uses the word *Gestell* to signify

> not so much the setting-up of an apparatus, as the set-up tout court, "the assigning or appointing of a definite place" (Webster's Unabridged: Globe Press, 1954). What is at stake is not the placing of something, but the staking out of place as such… The notion of emplacement… collects and assembles the various ways in which everything, human beings included, is 'cornered' (gestellt) and set in place. (pp. 988–989)

Heidegger explains that through this kind of technological setting up or emplacement, "nature reports itself in some way or other that is identifiable through calculation... it remains orderable as a system of information" (1992b, p. 304). Nature, the world around us, and even we as human beings, are collected and assembled by technologies in the form of information for calculation.

This description suits some aspects of computers and the online world rather well: By signing in and logging on, we can be said to identify ourselves and our subsequent actions online as orderable bits of data in a larger "system of information." We consequently become subject to various kinds of calculation and manipulation. As an extreme example, our identities and actions may be recorded in a marketer's or service provider's database, or more perniciously, may be intercepted by criminals. We may then be subject to manipulation in the form of unwanted email advertisements or become the object of cybercrime or identity theft.

Less extreme examples of this kind of calculation and identification are provided by the detailed tracking of student activities built into many online course management systems like Blackboard or Moodle. These systems provide "sophisticated, powerful, easy-to-use means of collecting data on students' activities within the learning space" (Land & Bayne, 2005, p. 165). The kinds of data collected and analyzed in these management systems include each student's logon times, the course Web pages they have visited, and the written communication they have viewed and composed (Land & Bayne, 2005, pp. 165–166). This information is then formatted and condensed in the form of reports that can be used by teachers for assessment purposes. Technology in this sense can be said to work subtly but also relentlessly to enframe or "set up" its human users.

In order to accomplish this goal, these information systems need to highlight certain quantifiable aspects of our identities and actions, and to downplay or ignore others. These systems, in other words, bring certain aspects to light, such as the *quantity* of time spent, and the *number* of pages or messages viewed; and at the same time, they remove other elements from attention or concern, such as the quality of the comments made or of the attention paid to each page or message. In providing the smallest details about the quantity of student activities, these information technologies make it easy for the teacher and student to focus on quantity rather than quality. This assessment does not mean, of course, that conscientious teachers and instructors cannot counteract this tendency of the technology. However, in order to do so, they must work not with patterns or systems of information and calculation, but in terms that are qualitative and experiential—terms, as we shall see throughout this book, that follow their own order and logic.

Computer and Internet technologies can be understood as opening up or "setting up" certain experiential opportunities or places, while "staking out" limitations on others. They make certain experiences, practices, and meanings possible and practical, while reducing the significance, purpose, and practicality of others. It is in these terms that the differences between online contexts and their face-to-face counterparts will be investigated in depth in this book. It is in these terms, in other words, that I will explore the "difference that makes a difference"—rather than more "insignificant" differences—for education face-to-face and online.

The purpose of this book, therefore, is to investigate the question of what is possible, what becomes difficult and what is perhaps no longer appropriate or plausible in the context of the "set-ups" that computers and network technologies bring with them. In working toward this purpose, I investigate the pedagogical significance of different places and spaces, online and offline, as well as the actions and the relationships that arise in them. I undertake this investigation by comparing online phenomena and their pedagogical significance to their counterparts offline. I will ask, in other words, how the "set-ups" of computers and technology can "stake out" or "enframe" places suitable for pedagogy. In so doing, I investigate whether and how pedagogical purposes and priorities can be cultivated in these locations and where it is that pedagogical relations readily flourish.

The intention, in short, is to question the "set-up" of computer and Internet technologies in education in relationship to "conventional" educational contexts. As indicated earlier, this process begins with setting up an open but unsettled question—a question that can now be formulated as follows:

*What are the differences separating screen and classroom as places or spaces
for pedagogy?*
By following the path that is opened up by this question, I will develop
and present an understanding of experiential and pedagogical differences
between the real and virtual. In doing so, my hope is *not* simply to arrive at "a
propositional statement about the matter at hand," but rather, to contribute
to "a transformation of thinking" about education and technology, and to
consider the implications this has for educational practice.

## Outline of the Book

In addressing the question of "the differences separating screen and classroom as spaces for pedagogy," it is first important to consider ways of thinking and investigating that would be appropriate to such a question. These
considerations are presented in the next chapter, entitled "Experiential
Evidence: I, We and You," which shows how different ways of approaching
experience are exemplified through the profound but everyday meanings
carried by the personal pronouns *I, we, it,* and *you.* In this chapter, I draw
attention to the relational and even ethical significance entailed in addressing another as "you," and to the sharing of meaning that can be realized in
saying "we." Saying "we" implies that there are aspects of meaning and experience that are more than merely individual and subjective, that are instead
*intersubjective.* In addition, I explain how these shared, commonly recognizable meanings are significant for my study overall. I also emphasize that these
ways of investigating experience and its meanings are rather different from
what is implied when we say the word "it": a more distanced, objectified and
objectifying way of speaking and thinking that is already well-represented
in research into online education.

The third chapter also takes language as its central theme. As I have
explained above, it is important to recognize the degree to which both established and new conceptualizations of technology and teaching are closely
tied to the language or vocabulary through which they are articulated. In
the third chapter, I therefore undertake to "unsettle" or put this language into
question. I do this by first surveying the highly figurative or metaphorical
language used to discuss computers and Internet in both everyday and specialized contexts. For example, these technologies are frequently labeled as

"cognitive tools" and "learning environments," and the students and teachers who engage with these systems are called "users" or "learners." I consider how such terminology communicates a promotional and above all instrumental bias, and I outline an alternative and more experientially attuned lexicon as an alternative.

In the chapters that follow, I put this alternative lexicon to use in an extended investigation of everyday pedagogical experiences, as they occur both online and in the classroom. This investigation is structured not in curricular or cognitive terms, but (as much as possible) using an experientially attuned vocabulary. One of the most important of these categories designates the experience of engaging with pedagogical *conditions*, *objects*, and *tasks*, both online and off, including those of reading and writing. In order to understand the pedagogical significance of online and offline places, it is necessary to explore the kinds of "virtual" and "real" books, pages, desktops, classrooms, seminars, and so on that are encountered in each. As I show in chapters four and five, these virtual and real entities and situations can have quite different experiential and pedagogical qualities.

In chapters six and seven, I undertake a similar investigation of a second significant type of experience: Experiences in which students encounter others. Given the social and relational character of pedagogical contexts, the way in which we engage with others online and offline is of paramount importance. As is the case in encounters with objects and situations, offline and online provide very different places for encountering others. The different experiential qualities of these encounters have far-reaching pedagogical implications. Focusing specifically on activities of classroom and online discussion in these chapters, I analyze how experiences of relation arise, both online and offline. I also give special attention to the complex and ambivalent (expressive, political, and performative) roles of our bodies in our everyday relations with others.

Through this investigation into pedagogical conditions and relations, I hope to make it clear that the way we experience and share the world, especially through our bodies, is of enormous and varied significance in pedagogical experience. The body, in other words, is particularly important in our relations with others, and it is in the contexts of embodied relation that significant differences between online and offline educational experience begin to appear. It is not so much that the body's non-verbal or paralinguistic cues are omitted online (as many conjecture, see preface), but rather that certain *contexts* associated with our embodiment are sharply attenuated or even eliminated online. I highlight a number of these embodied contexts by giving special attention, in chapters seven and eight, to the phenomenon of *silence*. The lived time, space, and relation associated with embodied silence serve as an important leverage point in this study, allowing me to identify further significant differences separating online and classroom education. Silence in online educational communication is generally regarded as a form of non-participation, and thus essentially as a "problem" to be "solved." Classroom silences, on the other hand, have been observed to be sometimes rich with pedagogical potential, and as I show, are closely related to the expressive and performative aspects of shared embodiment. In the eighth chapter, I develop these differences in terms of the ethics of the interpersonal encounter (and its own silences) that is articulated in the philosophy of Knud Løgstrup and Emmanuel Levinas. In this way, I am able to gradually lead the book to its conclusion by developing an account of educational practices and experiences as subject to a *relational* ethics—an ethics that comes to life when I am addressed by another as "you." Following Løgstrup and Levinas, this ethical pedagogical practice is exemplified *not* in the words of a contract or in images on the screen; it comes most fully to fruition in embodied contexts, in terms of what Levinas calls the "face."

Finally, I conclude the book by summarizing and synthesizing its findings, and also by articulating an answer to the question of spaces and places for pedagogy central to this book. This synthesis involves bringing into new combination many of the ideas and conclusions developed throughout the book. These conclusions do not prescribe a single, positive, instructional program or set of techniques, but rather, they point to a range of possible pedagogical practices. Indeed, these practices, correspondingly, are not about action and intervention as much as they are about receptivity, passivity, silence, and even unknowing.

# CHAPTER 2

# Experiential Evidence: I, We, and You

This book is motivated by the question of "the pedagogical significance of the relationships and spaces of the screen and the classroom." In the previous chapter, I emphasized how difficult this kind of question has proven for research in the past: the differences between the screen and the classroom, online and offline, have not been clarified through measures of teaching efficiency or learner performance, and can be confused through the language we use to describe these settings (e.g., speaking of "classrooms" and "discussions," both online and offline). At the same time, I emphasized that significant differences between screen and classroom *can* be registered *experientially.* To continue on our path questioning, in this chapter I ask: "How do we investigate this experience and from it, begin to understand the significance of the differences between online and offline?" This question requires a discussion of ways of coming to know *experience* and its meanings. In this chapter, I consider these issues in terms of four positions or perspectives evident in common language, and also implicit in the language of this book. These are:

1. The first-person perspective of the "I," which corresponds to *subjective* knowledge;
2. The second-person perspective of "you," which corresponds to *ethical* concerns;
3. The third-person perspective of "it" or "one," corresponding to *objective* knowledge;

4. The first-person plural perspective of "we," corresponding to *intersubjective* knowledge.[1]

I explore each of these perspectives and corresponding forms of knowledge in turn, focusing first on the subjective and objective (I and it), and then looking at the intersubjective (we) and finally, the ethical (you). In doing so, I sketch out a way in which experience can be studied, and its meanings can be interpreted.

To begin, consider again one of the descriptions of student experience that was provided at the outset of the previous chapter:

> *Imagine my surprise when I checked my blog the next day, and saw a comment from someone named Ari in Germany: "Nice story, Janet! I really like the fact that you got some help from others to get your project page done. I think this is very important in wikis." In the days that followed, Ari's comments boosted my confidence and motivated me to complete my first contribution to* Wikipedia.

This passage has many characteristics that make it potentially interesting and effective as an experiential description. One of the most important of these is the *perspective* from which it is told: Grammatically speaking, this is the perspective of the first person singular, of the "I": "Imagine *my* surprise when I checked *my* blog...." First person pronouns appear no less than seven times in this short passage. This description, then, is told from the position of the subject or "active participant," from what has been called the "inner-perspective" (Irrgang, 2007, pp. 23, 27). This is the perspective of subjective knowledge and personal impression. This is a position, for example, from which a person can say that he or she "really liked" something, or in which he or she can talk about having (or lacking) confidence and motivation to complete a difficult task. The position of the "I" has traditionally been taken as *the* starting point for certainty and knowledge overall. Descartes's famous phrase "I think; therefore I am" suggests that the thoughts I experience serve directly as the basis for the very existence of that "I." From this

........................................................................

1    I owe this particular account of personal perspectives and knowledge forms to Bernhard Irrgang; it is articulated briefly in the first chapter of *Gehirn und leiblicher Geist*, and was also discussed in the context of a series of seminars held at the Technical University Dresden in November of 2008. Related discussions of personal perspectives can be found in Zahavi 2005, Gainsford 2006, and Darwall, 2006. Martin Buber's *I and Thou* (1958) also deserves mention in this connection.

understanding, according to Descartes, should follow other certainties about myself and the world around me. However, this way of arriving at knowledge and certainty presents significant problems and challenges. Above all, this first-person knowledge is plagued by its potential to be "just" personal, idiosyncratic or arbitrary. That which is known in such a personal way may be private, or be kept as a kind of secret that is inaccessible to others. The relative "inaccessibility" of this subjective knowledge has led it to be derided as "merely" subjective, as capricious, biased, or idiosyncratic. Of course, this internal, subjective knowledge of the first person is in many ways the direct opposite of *objective* knowledge. Objective knowledge is thought to be independent from the subject or the "I," and is exemplified in the third-person perspective corresponding to the words "he/she/they," "it" or "one"). It is a position of the "onlooker" rather than of the active participant. It is the position, as Irrgang explains, of the "instrumentally-oriented... measuring observer," and is taken for granted as the objective or "natural" stance in the context of quantitative and scientific research (2007, p. 18). In its idealised form, this third-person knowledge is cleansed of any taint of the personal or subjective bias. Objective, independent knowledge of this kind is the operative mode in experimental research that attempts to establish generalizable or universal causal laws and interrelationships. It is gained not through subjective caprice, but by following rules and procedures that are unambiguous and unchanging. These rules and procedures are exemplified in scientific methods and measures that are meant to prove open, repeatable, and verifiable. They serve as a kind of ideal or paradigm for the type of research mentioned earlier that would measure the "statistically significant" difference caused by the introduction of technology in educational contexts. Unlike subjective, first-person knowledge, which is internal and even hidden, third-person objective knowledge is there for all to see. "Objective" realities and conditions persist or change independently, in apparent indifference to one's inner thoughts and feelings.

The perspectives of the subjective "I" and the objective "it" initially appear as mutually exclusive. Each is relatively independent of the other, and one cannot be reduced to the terms of the other. Feelings, impressions, or intimate secrets that may be constitutive of the "I" or self cannot simultaneously be explained away in objective terms. Feelings of pain (or pleasure) do not simply disappear by being accounted for in terms of nerve simulation and the brain's sensory receptors. Merleau-Ponty gives eloquent expression to the irreconcilability of these two ways of knowing in the preface to his *Phenomenology of Perception* (2002):

> I cannot conceive myself as nothing but a bit of the world, a mere object of biological, psychological or sociological investigation. I cannot shut myself up within the realm of science. All my knowledge of the world, even my scientific knowledge, is gained from my own particular point of view, or from some experience of the world without which the symbols of science would be meaningless. The whole universe of science is built upon the world as directly experienced... we must [therefore] begin by reawakening the basic experience of the world of which science is the second-order expression. (2002, p. ix)

The "I" appears intrinsically and irreconcilably opposed to the "it": The world of objectivity and science cannot shut subjectivity up within itself. The only way to understand "the precise meaning and scope" of science, Merleau-Ponty says, is "by reawakening the basic experience of the world" (p. viii). However, then the question is: Exactly how can this "reawakening" be achieved? Moreover, how can "the basic experience of the world" be brought to life without a retreat into the privacy of the "I"?

### Moving From I to We

One way to achieve this reawakening of experience is to recall that in addition to the "I" or "it" of the first- and third-person singular, it is also possible to say "we." Whereas "I" corresponds to the world of the subject and "it" (or he/she) to the world of the object, saying "we" opens up a way of knowing that is *inter*subjective. "We," as the first person plural, represents a kind of expansion of the subjectivity of the "I" across a plurality of first-person perspectives. Instead of designating a world of private, personal impressions and subjective knowledge, it refers to impressions and thoughts that can be shared and held in common by multiple subjectivities. This is the world of culture, both in the elevated sense of the arts, and in the everyday sense of social and cultural norms for speech and behavior.

The intersubjective "we" suggests that instead of being caught in an irreconcilable opposition between the objective and the subjective realm, there is a shared reality that is neither predominantly objective *nor* subjective. One way that the intersubjective realm is brought to life and to light is not through introspection exemplified in the "I" or through the objectivity of scientific investigation, but through *phenomenology* as both a methodology and a practice.[2] Writing again in the preface quoted above, Merleau-Ponty describes, in effect, how "I" becomes "we" in what he calls the intersubjective "phenomenological world":

> *The phenomenological world is… the sense which is revealed where the paths of my various experiences intersect, and also where my own and other people's intersect and engage each other like gears… It is thus inseparable from subjectivity and intersubjectivity, which find their unity when I either take up my past experiences in those of the present, or other people's in my own. … We witness every minute the miracle of related experiences, and yet nobody knows better than we do how this miracle is worked, for we are ourselves this network of relationships. (2002, p. xxii)*

Intersubjectivity, as Merleau-Ponty indicates, designates the intersection, "blending," or mutual conformity of plural subjectivities (2002, p. xii): "perspectives blend, perceptions confirm each other, a meaning emerges" (2002, p. xxii). The world that is experienced in this mutually engaged or convergent subjectivity is neither the private or inaccessible world of "inner-perspective," nor the immutable, indifferent world of the third-person objectivity. To express its unique experiential status, the phenomenological world of the "we" is called the "life-world:" a place where "extreme subjectivism and extreme objectivism" are overcome or "united" (2002, p. xxii). This phenomenological world is one that is available through a shared language, through collaborative action, and in common concerns.

This understanding is again illustrated in the two brief descriptive passages quoted at the outset of this book. Although both passages make use of

---

2   Phenomenology here designates what would be more accurately but more awkwardly termed "hermeneutic phenomenology." Referring to the art and science of interpretation, hermeneutics has been combined with phenomenology to constitute an interpretation or investigation of the *meaning* of lived experience. Exemplary treatments of hermeneutic phenomenology can be found in the writings of Martin Heidegger and Hans-Georg Gadamer.

the "I" perspective of personal feelings and impressions (rather than explicitly saying "we"), each of the two descriptions exemplifies how such personal perspectives intersect or, as Merleau-Ponty (2002) says, constitute a "closely woven fabric" (p. xi). In the case of the first description, it is the student's and teacher's perspectives that intersect in an exchange of glances and of questions and answers. Ultimately, the sharing between the two allows the student to feel "relaxed and smart" with the teacher. In the case of the second description, Janet and Ari's interactions also show how different "people's [experiences] intersect and engage each other like gears" (Merleau-Ponty, 2002, p. xxii): Ari from Germany tells Janet how much he likes the fact that she got help from others. In fact, these comments boost Janet's confidence, motivating her to complete her first article on *Wikipedia*. These two descriptions show, in other words, how the shared life-world is one where it is certainly possible to say "I," and to have feelings and impressions of one's own. Further, it also reflects a context in which the first-person pronoun is constituted through its relation with others. Using the "we" or the intersubjective first-person plural perspective himself, Merleau-Ponty puts it this way:

> We *witness every minute the miracle of related experiences, and yet nobody knows better than* we *do how this miracle is worked, for* we *are ourselves this network of relationships. The world and reason are not problematical. We may say, if we wish, that they are mysterious, but their mystery defines them: there can be no question of dispelling it by some "solution"* (2002, p. xxiii, emphases added)

The *we* represents more than one I; *we* connects multiple subjectivities through common concerns and feelings, impressions and meanings that are shared in common.

At the same time, though, the word "we" presents challenges: it has been described by some as a "dangerous pronoun" that is sometimes associated with the suppression of difference and even with acts of hate (e.g., Moss, 2003). Peppers (2006) explains that *we* "is a dangerous pronoun when it hides histories of internal conflict under false or superficial commonality." Leaving little or no opportunity for confirmation or qualification, saying "we" in a text often simply assumes that the reader is a part of the superficial agreement. It tacitly but unmistakably asks the reader to align himself or herself with the "I" of the author. In doing so tacitly or implicitly—rather than forthrightly or explicitly—it does not readily allow for conflict and disagreement. By using "we" in this book, I am aware of this dilemma. However, I also believe that it can be addressed, not always fully or completely, but in the ethical terms that are proper to it, through the use of the second-person pronoun, "you." I, therefore, return to this issue in the last section of this chapter, where I consider the ethical implications of saying "you."

## Dimensions of Life-World Experience

The study of the experience of classroom and screen undertaken in this book is, in effect, an exploration of a small part of the shared life-world. Exploring this intersubjective realm involves particular techniques that combine elements of inner and outer subjectivity and objectivity. One of these techniques is to understand life-world experience as extending or unfolding along four axes, dimensions or "existentials." These life-world dimensions have wide applicability (without being simply "objective") and are also closely connected to the expression of feelings and impressions (without being reduced to "mere" subjectivity). Working in complex inter-mixture, these dimensions are a part of the way that life-world experience is organized, or inherent in the way we "live in" or inhabit the life-world. Consequently, they are designated as "lived space," "lived time," "lived body," and "lived relation."

*Lived space*, of course, is *not* the objective area measured by the square feet in a room or kilometers of distance to be traveled; it is instead the way that a room or a distance is lived in or experienced: as warm and inviting, as conveniently nearby or unreachably distant. Max van Manen (2002) characterizes this life-world dimension as follows:

> this space is... *difficult to put into words since the experience of lived space (like that of lived time or body) is largely pre-verbal; we do not ordinarily reflect on it. And yet we know that the space in which we find ourselves affects the way we feel. The huge spaces of a modern bank building may make us feel small, the wide-open space of a landscape may make us feel exposed but also*

*possibly free. And we may feel just the opposite when we get in a crowded elevator. (n.p.)*

"In general," van Manen concludes, "we may say that we *become* the space we are in" (2002; emphasis added). Given the importance of place and space in this inquiry into the place of the classroom and the space of the screen, this life-world dimension is referenced consistently throughout this book.

*Lived time* is similar to the existential dimension of lived space: it is *not* "objective" time measured through the indifferent units presented on a clock or calendar, but it is the experience of time as something colored by our own lives. It can "speed up when we enjoy ourselves," or slow down "when we feel bored …or when we… sit anxiously in the dentist's chair" (van Manen, 2002). Significantly, it becomes inextricably intertwined with the experience of space in a monotonously long journey or in a pleasant stroll.

*Lived body* correspondingly refers to the experience of our own bodies and those of others. Of course, this experience can be sexual or erotic in character, but more often than not, it is banal or at least ambiguous. The body can be the object of another's scrutinizing gaze, in which case it also often becomes an object of awkward self-awareness. It can be comfortable or uncomfortable, but it often disappears from awareness altogether when engaged in an absorbing task. It communicates and connects with others in powerful but elusive ways. We may be particularly aware of this power when we are trying to create a favorable impression on someone: folding one's hands behind one's back (instead of crossing them on one's chest) to communicate openness, or inching backward as an expression of discomfort or unease. As van Manen notes, "in our physical or bodily presence we both reveal something about ourselves and we conceal something at the same time—not necessarily consciously or deliberately, but rather in spite of ourselves" (1997, p. 103).

*Lived relation* refers to the everyday experience of other people, or more abstractly, of the "other." Just as we experience time, space and the body in forms that are colored by emotion and impression, so too do we "live" our relations with others in terms that are charged with feeling, texture, and even flavor. This scenario is illustrated in the language we use to describe our relationships and encounters: "She's a prickly person," "he gives me the creeps," "she's always very sweet," or "that certainly leaves a bitter taste in my mouth!" These kinds of expressions show that we experience relation deeply and even sensuously (in terms of taste and tactility), rather than in more objective, intellectual terms. Lived relation, along with lived space, is the second of the four life-world dimensions to be invoked in the title of this book and is correspondingly one of the most important of the life-world dimensions in this study. It is also the most challenging to observe and analyze.

Significant aspects of all of these four life-world dimensions—as well as other life-world characteristics—are illustrated in many of the chapters of this book. These dimensions can be said to "organize" the life-world, and they can also be seen as organizing my analyses in this book. In each chapter, there is generally a primary experiential dimension that receives explicit descriptive and interpretive attention, and a secondary dimension that emerges more implicitly.

TABLE 1: *Life-World Dimensions and their Analysis in this Text*

| SECTION/ CHAPTER | PHENOMENA | PRIMARY LIFE-WORLD DIMENSION(S) | SECONDARY LIFE-WORLD DIMENSION(S) |
|---|---|---|---|
| II/Chapter 4 | Basic conditions of the classroom and screen | Time, Space | Body |
| II/Chapter 5 | Objects and "quasi-others" | Body | Relation to Others |
| III/Chapter 6 | Others in discussion | Body | Relation to Others |
| III/Chapter 7 | Encountering the other | Relation to Others | Body |

As this table indicates, the general focus of this book begins with our involvement with objects and contexts, and moves to an analysis of our encounters and engagements with others. In doing so, it starts off with an emphasis on the life-world dimensions of time and space, and moves through a sustained focus on the lived body to finally concentrate on the dimension of relation.

### Experience as Information or Event

Speaking specifically of *experience* in terms of the dimensions of lived time, space, relation, and embodiment implies a perhaps uncommon way of understanding the term. Experience is often seen as being grounded in sense data, in "information" that is first received through the five senses, and then given "sense" by being "processed," organized, and analyzed in the mind. As I mentioned in the preface to this book, this particular understanding of experience is sometimes associated with *empiricism*. Empiricism refers to the belief that knowledge arises primarily or exclusively through the senses and, ultimately, that

> *experience is only a matter of data, sense data to be sure but data nonetheless. Considered this way experience is nothing more than a basic component of knowledge that completes itself only through an act of reason, that is, in the establishing of patterns, of generalizations… it is something [that] stands within the framework of calculation and repeatability. (Risser, 2010, n. p.)*

It is precisely in terms of generalization, calculation, and repeatability that the word experience has been used in recent discussions of computer technology and online education. In all cases, experience of users and learners is seen as a feature that is largely subject to manipulation, measurement, and optimization. In some circles, the design of human-computer interfaces (H C I), for example, has been re-christened "user experience" (U X) design, with books on "designing the… user experience" and "measuring the user experience" having recently appeared (Ginsburg, 2010; Tullis & Albert, 2010). In online education in particular, experience—above all learner or student experience—tends to be understood in similar terms, via automatically generated records of online student activity and interactivity (e.g., Heckman & Annabi, 2003), or as a function of student satisfaction, performance, and attrition (e.g., Chiu, Stewart, & Ehlert, 2003, Picciano, 2002; see also the review of Hiltz & Shea, 2005, pp. 149–156). One study, for example, speaks of "instructors and administrators" being able to use a set of standards to "measure various aspects of the distance education experience and their importance to students" (e.g., Jurczyk, Kushner-Benson, & Savery, 2004). As in the literature of "user experience," these educationally relevant "aspects of experience" are "measured" through the use of questionnaires that present students with preset questions and question types, including multiple choice, Likert-scale, sentence completion, ordinal ranking, and others (e.g., Burgess, 2001, pp. 8–10). Student experiences, correspondingly, are predefined in terms of degrees of favorable or unfavorable response, or of a predetermined set of characteristics of a course or program, its delivery, and measures of its ultimate outcomes.

In the context of phenomenology, however, experience is seen very differently: It is not understood in terms of the accumulation and synthesis of sensory data that can be measured through multiple-choice questions and answers, or as an image designed or manipulated on a computer screen. It is not about information, but it is understood in terms of an event. It is not a picture we design, gather, or piece together, but it is a phenomenon that occurs, takes place, or happens to us. "The crucial question" for phenomenology, in other words, is "not 'what do I experience?' but 'what is my experience?'" (Jay, 2006, p. 94). Experience, accordingly, is not an occurrence that happens outside of us, as something separate from us that is made to impinge upon us. As Heidegger says, "Experience doesn't pass before me as thing that I set there as an object" (as quoted in Jay, 2006, p. 98). Experience instead is a part of the inseparable connections between the self and the world. It arises through engagement with the world of concerns, actions, and meanings that constitute the life-world. Experience, conceived in this way, is a part of the life-world that we inhabit "naturally" and it partakes in all of the characteristics of this life-world. As Gadamer (2004) explains,

> the world in which we are immersed in the natural attitude . . . never becomes
> an object as such for us, but that represents the pregiven basis of all experience.
> . . . It is clear that the life-world is always at the same time a communal world
> that involves being with other people as well. It is a world of persons, and in
> the natural attitude the validity of this personal world is always assumed.
> (p. 239)

To put it another way, experience is embedded in the life-world, and because this world, as Gadamer points out, is a "communal world of persons," experience is always much more than a question of unidirectional manipulation and calculation.

Taking this idea even further, one could say that we do not possess our experience, our experience possesses us. Heidegger expresses this concept by saying that

> To undergo an experience with something... means that this something befalls us, strikes us, comes over us, overwhelms us, and transforms us. When we talk of "undergoing" an experience we mean specifically that the experience is not of our making. To undergo here means that we endure it, suffer it, receive it as it strikes us, and submit to it. (1971, p. 57)

Heidegger's conclusion that "experience is not of our making"—taken together with the notion that we submit to it, rather than it submitting to us—is precisely how experience is understood here. Far from being subject to design and measurement, experience is seen as an event that is always embedded in a life-world of other persons.

## Space Versus Place

Up to this point, in discussing life-world experience and the ways it befalls us, I have used the terms *space* and *place* more or less interchangeably. However, these two words carry with them their own phenomenological or experiential meanings, which require further exploration. Writing in *Space and Place: The Perspective of Experience* (2001), Yi-Fu Tuan observes that

> "Space" and "place" are familiar words denoting common experiences. We live in space. There is no space for another building on the lot. The Great Plains look spacious. Place is a security, space is freedom: we are attached to the one and long for the other. There is no place like home. What is home? It is the old homestead, the old neighborhood, hometown or motherland. Geographers study places. Planners would like to evoke a "sense of place". These are unexceptional ways of speaking. Space and place are basic components of the lived world; we take them for granted. When we think about them, however, they may assume unexpected meanings and raise questions we have not thought to ask. (p. 3)

Space and place, as Tuan indicates, can be differentiated according to everyday language and to the experiences that are part of this language. Thus, home can be said to be not nearly as much a *space* as it is a *place*. An airplane, cruising at 30,000 feet, travels through *space*, but can be said ultimately to be taking its passengers to a particular *place*. Space, in other words, is the distance covered on the map, and place is the final destination. From the empty void of *space*, astronauts have been reported as seeing the green white and blue sphere of the earth as home, as a precious *place* of origin. Although their meanings are similar, the words space and place are not readily interchangeable in sentences like the ones above. Exchanging their position or role would render the examples awkward and problematic: Just as an airplane in the sky, to take this one example, is not in any one "place," its passengers would generally not say they have a particular "space" as their destination.

Meanings of space and place, as Tuan points out, rely on "each other for definition." As the examples above show, "place" he says, "is pause" whereas "space" is "that which allows movement" (2001, p. 6). Place, in other words, is associated with stasis and rest, and space with action and mobility. Each "pause in movement" in space, Tuan says, "makes it possible for location to be transformed into place" (p. 6). Place, in other words, is a particular, unique location where one pauses. Space, on the other hand, provides a means of moving and getting there—the more open and accommodating this motion is, the more truly spatial and spacious it becomes. The movement, freedom, and action that space facilitate can be localized through gradual processes of personalization and habituation, eventually allowing it to acquire the status of place: "What begins as undifferentiated space" Tuan explains, can become a "place as we get to know it better and endow it with value" (p. 6). Such features give locations that might otherwise seem only suited to a single, relatively placeless function, the attributes that Tuan assigns to place. As Tuan explains, "enclosed and humanized space[s]," whatever their purpose, end up being "place" (p. 54).

> *Space is a common symbol of freedom in the Western world. Space lies open; it suggests the future and invites action. On the negative side, space and free-dom are a threat... Open space has no trodden paths and signposts. It has no fixed pattern of established human meaning; it is like a blank sheet on which meaning may be imposed. Enclosed and humanized space is place. Compared*

> *to space, place is a calm center of established values. Human beings require*
> *both space and place. Human lives are a dialectical movement between shelter*
> *and venture, attachment and freedom. In open space one can become intensely*
> *aware of place; and in the solitude of a sheltered place the vastness of space*
> *beyond acquires a haunting presence. (p. 54)*

Space and place represent opposed but interdependent categories for classifying and understanding our experience of "lived space." Tuan's characterizations of place as home and as rest correspond to the lived experiences of a warm and inviting location or locale; and his descriptions of space correspond to the monotonous distances that must be covered by the traveler. It might therefore be more accurate to speak of the dimension of "lived space and place." As Tuan says, lived experiences of places and spaces are interdependent and interconnected. The comfort of home is often no more intensely experienced than after a long trip, to a distant place.

In his comprehensive text *Getting Back Into Place*, philosopher Edward Casey develops the distinction between space and place in a slightly different direction:

> *By "space" is meant a neutral, pre-given medium, a tabula rasa onto which*
> *the particularities of a culture and a history come to be inscribed, with place*
> *as the presumed result. [It is the] idea of... a "sheer physical terrain"... of an*
> *"existential space"...a "blank environment" [which] ... entails that to begin*
> *with there is some empty and innocent spatial spread, waiting, as it were for*
> *cultural configurations to render it placeful. (2009, p. 318)*

Casey is emphasizing here the affinity between space and abstract, conceptual locations or extensions. Place, correspondingly for Casey, as for Tuan, is a "given," and it is "concrete." Space can be understood, in other words, not only as a place of motion, but also as a kind of absolute and abstract emptiness or blankness that exists in the mind of a geographer, astronomer, or philosopher. Space extends to the kind of abstract, purely conceptual forms of extension and location that are a part of what Husserl referred to as "mathematics and mathematical science." Such a purely conceptual realm, from the perspective of phenomenology, can only be understood as arising from, and being ultimately reducible to the terms and palpability of the life-world. This type of abstract space, in other words, forms a kind of "garb of ideas, or … garb of symbols," which, as Husserl says, can only be used to represent or to dress up the life-world as "objectively actual and true." Such abstract and ideational space, it follows, is in a sense beyond the reach of place; it cannot be emplaced, even though it is ultimately dependent on place for its invention and origin. To enter into the life-world, it must become something quite different—something concrete and irreplaceable.

## Writing and Reading the Life-World

The four life-world dimensions, time, body, space (and/or place,) and relation are bound together by and reflected in everyday language. Indeed, whether it is used in careful description or casual conversation, language is the most common means through which, as Merleau-Ponty says, "perspectives blend, perceptions confirm each other, a meaning emerges" (p. xix). Language provides the most powerful evidence for the existence of a shared life-world; correspondingly, it also forms the most effective tool for exploring it. The simple fact that we can understand one another when speaking of different aspects of experience, feeling, and meaning, is a clear illustration of a shared, intersubjective world.

This dynamic gives language a particular power or potential in phenomenological research. This aspect is the potential of the "evocation" or even the "simulation" of experience. More specifically, this power is illustrated in the two descriptive passages that open the first chapter of this book. Writing, for example, that "my teacher… looks at me with this particular humours glance" or that "Ari's comments boosted my confidence" show the potential of descriptive and everyday writing to present an experiential moment to the reader. Longer and more detailed passages have the potential to extend this power and to draw the reader into an experience, to evoke an experience for the reader, or even to enable the reader to "experience" it vicariously. Realizing this potential involves the use of linguistic or descriptive techniques that are closer to fictional writing than they are to the objective "third-person" forms of description. It involves writing, in other words, that draws from the shared subjective and personal experiential characteristics that constitute the common world of the "we" rather than the objective world of factual or academic texts. These techniques, in turn, are intended to give the reader the opportunity to "participate" in the experience described, to become part of the plurality that is implied in the word "we."

There are other similarities linking this type of description to fictional writing: A novel and its characters and events, for example, can lie dormant on the shelf, to be given semblance of life when the novel is picked up and read. Descriptions used in phenomenological research are similarly dependent on the reader. The reader is asked to help "breathe life" into these descriptions, to encounter these passages with the expectation and sensibility of someone reading fiction, from an orientation of involved receptivity rather than analytic detachment. Of course, this approach is by no means an appeal for the reader to abandon all possibility of independent disagreement or critique. What these kinds of descriptions instead ask for is a similar kind of reading to that of engaging in a work of fiction or viewing a motion picture.

The word "I" is accordingly used in these descriptions in a manner similar to the way it would be used in fictional passages written in the first person. It is not meant to emphasize the inward-looking or introspective possibilities of selfhood, but rather, is an attempt to make the descriptions as direct, recognizable, and compelling as possible, and to encourage the overlapping of different first-person perspectives. This book, at other points, like Merleau-Ponty (above) and Husserl (just below), also uses the word "we" in a similar manner, to invoke the intersubjective position of the third-person plural. The study of the experience of classroom and screen undertaken in this book, then, is an exploration of the shared life-world that is invoked or simulated through descriptive, evocative language. However, while this "sharing" of a common life-world is an important goal, the ultimate aim of this study is even more ambitious: To bring these shared experiences and meanings to explicit and reflective attention. In doing so, this study aims to more than just describe, it also aims to reflect upon and interpret these descriptions. The book alternates between descriptive passages (which are indented and italicized in the text) and writing that is reflective and interpretive in character.

Despite its unconventional ambiguity and informality, this type of inquiry can be both valuable and accessible: As I have already demonstrated, it can address familiar issues and questions in ways that are quite different from conventional research. This method can be particularly valuable in cases where conventional research has asked the same question again and again, only to repeatedly receive the same answers.

## Phenomenological Description and the Utrecht School

The quasi-fictional descriptive method explained above was initially conceived in the context of the Dutch Utrecht School and has been developed further and given explicit articulation by Max van Manen, a Canadian educational researcher. This section provides an overview of the way that evidence is collected and then presented and analyzed through writing, using the method of phenomenological description, as developed by van Manen and used in this book. The Utrecht school, which flourished only for a decade or so (from 1946 to 1957), represented a loose grouping of scholars who applied aspects of phenomenology as a research method to a wide range of disciplines. Writing together with Utrecht scholar Bas Levering, van Manen explains:

> The Utrecht School consisted of an assortment of phenomenologically oriented psychologists, educators, pedagogues, pediatricians, sociologists, criminologists, jurists, psychiatrists, and other medical doctors, who formed a more or less close association of like-minded academics. (Levering & van Manen, 2003, p. 278)

In recent years, as van Manen observes, the work of this group "...has inspired...variations of a practice-based phenomenology especially in psychology (e.g., Giorgi [2009] and Moustakas [1994]), in nursing (e.g., Benner [1994]) and in education (e.g., van Manen)" (2002).

One of the notable characteristics of the work of the Utrecht School is the way its members would "write up" their research in an informal, even conversational way. The research publications that are most characteristic of this school skillfully interweave informal descriptive writing with more formal reflection and analysis. This task was accomplished so successfully in some cases that the careful and painstaking research, writing and re-writing efforts of the authors are difficult for the reader to detect. In addition, these researchers did not produce any writings that explicated their methodology. Thus, despite the existence of some exemplary pieces associated with the Utrecht School (e.g., Langeveld, 1983; Buytendijk, 1988; Bleeker & Mulderij, 1992), the very accessibility of the writing of these texts effectively "closed the possibility for others to exercise these same practices" (Levering & van Manen, 2003, p. 278). The apparent simplicity of accomplished writing, in other words, all too easily hid the complexity of the research processes beneath it.

In this context, van Manen's work can be characterized as an attempt to "reopen" the possibility of exercising these same practices of research and writing for others. In *Researching Lived Experience: Human Science for an Action Sensitive Pedagogy* (1997), van Manen explains in some detail how researchers can work toward the close and apparently effortless interweaving of analysis, reflection, and informal description that typifies the texts of the Utrecht School. In this same book, van Manen also explains how to collect, combine, and refine interview and other descriptive material to serve as experiential data in this kind of research. As the title of van Manen's book indicates, pedagogy is a subject particularly germane to this type of research.

"Phenomenology," as van Manen says, "is the active and reflective participation in meaning" (2002). The phenomenological researcher in this sense does not typically have a data gathering phase with an explicit beginning and ending set in advance but instead "dwells" with his or her question as it is being formulated, while he or she may be away from her desk and studies, during formal interviewing and analysis activities, and throughout the writing process. A film, a novel, or a radio program may suddenly speak to the researcher and the question with which she is dwelling, shedding light on one aspect or another of the phenomenon in question. As a result, it is often not possible to give an exhaustive account of data sources or even a clear-cut enumeration of a single sample set or collection of interviews. It would be in some ways more in the spirit of the research method to describe the relevant contexts and experiences engaged in while dwelling with the problem.

The sources of potential meaning or relevant data are numerous. The researcher can develop and cultivate experiential meaning as it arises in a range of sources, including "historical, cultural, literary" and aesthetic materials (e.g., historical accounts, novels, and films), as well as a range of linguistic sources, including metaphors, sayings, and etymological and definitional distinctions both from everyday speech and formal writing (2002).

For example, a popular movie such as *You've Got Mail* (1998) has been used in one hermeneutic phenomenological investigation of "keeping in touch by electronic mail" (Dobson, 2002), just as descriptions of working at a computer or typewriter, and fictional accounts of reading and writing in and outside of class, are central to my analyses below.

These sources are used to create the types of first-person, written descriptions discussed above. When these descriptions are carefully developed and refined to constitute short, self-contained, quasi-fictional accounts, they are referred to by van Manen as "anecdotes." The anecdote as van Manen defines it is a brief, simple story, a vividly particular presentation of a single incident that is intended to stand out precisely through its incidental nature, in its compressed but concrete particularity. Again, the two very short descriptions that opened the first chapter of this book can be considered as exemplary— if rather compressed—anecdotes: they are very particular and concrete; they focus, however briefly, on a specific incident, whether it is the characteristic look of a teacher (and a student's response to it) or the encouraging effect of kind words from a far-away collaborator. Both present an everyday kind of event and experience, highlighting one aspect that stands out for the person involved in it. Further examples of anecdotes and "anecdotal-styled" description are provided and interpreted in sections two and three of this book.

The term *anecdote* has been deliberately chosen by van Manen for its colloquial overtones and its obvious distance from any validated and authoritative sense of "truth" or "evidence":

> *Anecdotes have enjoyed low status in scholarly writings... Evidence that is "only anecdotal" is not permitted to furnish a proper argument. But empirical generalization is not the aim of phenomenological research. [In fact, anecdotes]... express a certain distain for the alienated and alienating discourse of scholars who have difficulty showing how life and theoretical propositions are connected. (p. 119)*

It is useful also to characterize an anecdote can by what it is *not*: it does not present general principles, statistical patterns, or theoretical constructs. It is not used as evidence in the sense of an historical incident that "really happened" at a given point in time. Thus, an anecdote can be "adapted" from another text or description, as is the case with the second short anecdote provided at the outset of chapter one. The anecdote should also be differentiated from the vivid ethnographic accounts of computer use of the kind provided by Sherry Turkle in *The Second Self* (1984, 2005) or *The Life on the Screen* (1995), which Turkle (2005) characterizes as "portraits of what can [and does] happen when people enter into very close relationships" with the computer (p. 25). When employed as a means of studying engagement with computer technology, anecdotal accounts generally do not serve as evidence of what can happen with this technology. Instead, they attempt to provide the reader with recognizable experiences of this kind of engagement. Anecdotes are not presented to the reader with the tacit claim, "This really happened"; they instead bring with them the tacit appeal: "Is this experientially recognizable or resonant?" More specifically then, the anecdote is told with the intention of raising the further question: "What is the experiential meaning of what happened?"

Despite the reach and variety of potential sources in writing anecdotes and in carrying out phenomenological research, the principle supply of meaning or of experiential data is often presented by open-ended, "qualitative" interviews. As a data-gathering technique generally, this type of interview is marked by its unstructured and unscripted nature. One of the most important challenges in such an interview is not for the interviewer to stick to a particular script, but for him or her to remain responsive, "flexible and attentive to the... meanings that may emerge as the interview progresses" (Warren, 2002, p. 87). Such an interview also tends to take the form of a kind of an "interpretive" or "guided conversation" that unfolds with very few pre-determined questions. It relies on the unscripted use of "probes to clarify answers or [to] request further examples, and follow-up questions that pursue implications of answers to main questions" (van Manen, 2002; Warren, 2002, pp. 85, 86–87).

Using the term *hermeneutic interview* (1997, pp. 98–99; 2002) van Manen describes the point of such an interview as follows:

> A hermeneutic interview is an interpretive conversation wherein both partners reflectively orient themselves to the interpersonal or collective ground that brings the significance of the phenomenological question into view. The art

*of the researcher in the hermeneutic interview is to keep the question (of the*
*meaning of the phenomenon [under investigation]) open: to keep himself or*
*herself and the interviewee oriented to the substance of the thing being ques-*
*tioned. (2002, n.p.)*

In the course of such an interview, it is important for the researcher to be on the lookout for descriptive material having potentially anecdotal or "quasi-fictional" qualities. These brief descriptions take the form of a short account or a notable or unusual incident that captures or says something about the experience or phenomenon in question.

Interviewing in phenomenological research often presents a number of significant challenges. The first of these is that participants or interviewees generally do not see experiential categories as being relevant in research contexts; they do not describe their experience in terms of "incidents" or according to an experientially attuned vocabulary. To help both interviewee and interviewer to maintain a focus on the experiential, it can be useful to employ certain ways of asking questions or setting up "probes" that guide the conversation away from theory and explanation and keep it firmly anchored in the concrete. One of these ways is to explore the experience with the interviewee in terms of the four fundamental life-world themes or dimensions: lived space, lived time, lived relation, and lived body. A second way of addressing this difference is to ask questions that lead the interviewer to switch from a conventional vocabulary of intellection and thought to one of feeling and impression. Thus, asking a question like "what did you *think* when that happened" would be replaced with the question: "how did you *feel* when that happened?" Allowing participants to speak in terms of thinking and of the intellect can provide responses that may, in effect, theorize colloquially the phenomenon in question. On the other hand, focusing the participant on his or her feelings and responses can help to orient and open the interview to questions of situated attunement and "dwelling."

In keeping with the implications of "dwelling" with a question and data, the data gathered from the participant or interviewee in phenomenological research is typically not seen as coming to an end with the conclusion of the initial interview session. Van Manen encourages researchers to include participants in the ongoing, cyclical, hermeneutic development of experiential meanings as these unfold in subsequent stages in the research. This dynamic includes discussing interview notes or interview transcripts with the interviewee and exploring together themes or important, common meanings that might emerge from these provisional documents. Involvement of the interviewee also extends to the review and discussion of more developed and refined descriptive material and drafts of the research text itself. According to van Manen, the question "Is this what the experience is really like?" should ground all such discussions (2002).

### Wonder Versus the "Natural Attitude"

Gathering, compiling, writing and re-writing descriptions in order to make aspects of the life-world clearly available for reflection is not easy; for what is often most noteworthy about the world of shared human meanings is precisely the fact that it is *not usually regarded as worthy of note.* In this section, I introduce a few concepts that are indispensable to the type of phenomenological research discussed in this book: natural attitude, intentionality, and wonder (the last of these is also known as "the reduction"). Our sharing of everyday meanings and the overlapping of common experiences is something that is readily forgotten, overlooked, or ignored. One could say that we are to the life-world as a fish is to water: The life-world is the environment that surrounds and sustains us, but because it is everywhere, it tends to be the last thing to receive our notice. Consequently, we are not often in a good position to explore it or even to acknowledge its reality. It disappears all too easily between the opposed domains of the objective and the subjective. Edmund Husserl explains:

> the lifeworld, for us who wakingly live in it, is always there, existing in advance for us, the 'ground' of all praxis, whether theoretical or extratheoretical. The world is pregiven to us, the waking, always somehow practically interested subjects, not occasionally but always and necessarily as the universal field of all actual and possible praxis, as horizon. To live is always to live-in-certainty-of-the-world. (1970, p. 142)

"Living-in-certainty-of-the-world" generally comes to explicit attention only when an extraordinary event occurs—when the figurative "gears" mentioned by Merleau-Ponty become disengaged. Such an event may occur when travelling in a foreign country or entering for the first time into a situation that is very different or "other" from what is familiar: we are confronted by practices or conventions that may violate our "living-in-certainty-of-the-world" or our unarticulated "common sense."

An important constituent of this commonsensical "living in certainty" is called "intentionality." Intentionality refers to the meanings, plans, and purposes that constitute our connection with the world around us and give the world its familiarity. Extending from unconscious habits and actions (like turning a page or clicking a link) through to the most complex tasks of focused (self-)awareness, intentionality designates to a kind of "directionality" that links self to the world:

> "Intentionality" derives from the Latin verb "intendere", which means "to point to" or "to aim at," and … the intentionality of mental states and experiences… [are] accordingly characterized… [as] being "directed toward something"… i.e., a mental state of "aiming" toward a certain state of affairs. (McIntyre & Woodruff Smith, 1989, p. 147)

While phenomenological research begins with the recognition that self and world are connected through intentionality, it focuses particular attention on those moments when intentionality is disrupted. When the purposive powers of the mind are disrupted, miss their target, or are exposed to strangeness or otherness, the completion of intended actions comes to a halt. Merleau-Ponty speaks of phenomenology as working to encourage these moments. He describes it as an attempt to "slacke[n] the intentional threads which attach us to the world and thus [bring] them to our notice…" (2002, p. xv). Slackening is deliberately cultivated as part of a particular methodology or technique, or more accurately, as an attitude or *disposition.* This technique or attitude is known as "the reduction." The reduction refers to the suspension of both commonsense and scientific understandings or explanations. Husserl describes it as "the bracketing" of the "natural attitude." Cultivating this disposition or sensitivity to that which is "out of the ordinary" is central to the research, writing, and re-writing that have occurred in putting a study or a book like this together. However, it is crucial in reading such a study as well.

The highest goal of the writing and reflection undertaken here is to remove the reader as far as possible from what Husserl has called the "natural attitude." The ultimate aim of this book in this sense is to bring the reader to a place where the phenomena being investigated are no longer simply taken for granted and accepted as ordinary. The goal is to take the reader to a place where the natural attitude is suspended; ultimately to a place of wonder. As van Manen (2002) explains, the goal of the type of phenomenological writing practiced here is to

> *shatter the taken-for-grantedness of our everyday reality. Wonder [in this sense] is the unwilled willingness to meet what is utterly strange in what is most familiar. It is the willingness to step back and let things speak to us, a passive receptivity to let the things of the world present themselves in their own terms. When we are struck with wonder, our minds are suddenly cleared of the clutter of everyday concerns that otherwise constantly occupy us. We are confronted by the thing, the phenomenon in all of its strangeness and unique-ness. The wonder of that thing takes us in… (n.p.)*

To respond to a text with wonder, to meet the "utterly strange" in a phenom-enon that may be otherwise thoroughly "known" and familiar, however, is to ask a great deal of both the researcher/writer and the reader. Reacting in this fashion is not automatic, and, of course, it cannot be forced. As a result my intention or hope is therefore to *invite*, rather than in any way to compel, the reader into a suspension of the mundane. To extend this invitation to the reader is to ask him or her to enter into a different personal perspective, that of the "you," of the relational and the ethical. Only in this way is it ultimately possible to share the world of the "we."

## Saying "You" and the Ethics of Address

The relational, ethical aspects of the first-person plural perspective become important, even unavoidable, when we address someone as "you." In say-ing "you," the person speaking offers, establishes, or elaborates a relation to the person addressed. "You" implies relation; it is a word spoken by an "I" to another. When Ari says to Janet, "I really like the fact that you got some help from others to get your project page done. I think this is very important in wikis," he is engaged in relational action that has clearly ethical implications: his figurative path intersects (to use Merleau-Ponty's terms) with Janet's in a way that affects her noticeably and meaningfully. As a result, Ari's address or relational action can also be interpreted in terms of what is good or bad, right or wrong: The effect of Ari's words on Janet might lead readers to conclude that it was the *right* thing to say or do. A different response or a different end result—for example, appearing to be too enthusiastic, leading Janet to question Ari's seriousness—might result in a different ethical judgement.

The "you" perspective is relevant to the methodology of this book because the descriptive and interpretive passages in this book have been written with the intention of addressing the reader individually, as an "I" would address a "you." In writing this book then, I am aiming, ideally, to bring the reader to the text in a "you" relation with me. Together the two, the you and the I, *may* form an intersubjective "we." This dynamic implies that "I" as author has an ethical responsibility in relation to "you" as the reader.

This responsibility can be best understood in linguistic terms because language not only has substantial power to suggest, evoke, and simulate; it also presents significant peril in that it can mislead and, above all, reinforce the "natural attitude" that does not see beyond received common sense. As indicated above, my aim in writing is not to use language and description to compel readers to arrive at certain experiential meanings and understandings; my aim instead is to invite readers to share a range of experiential possibilities. Such an invitation is intended when I use the sometimes dangerous first-person pronoun "we": I do not do so without acknowledging the suppositions that this word brings with it, and the power it has to cover over conflict and disagreement with a superficial sense of commonality. Thus, I simultaneously invite the reader to disagree with what is suggested when I use the term *we* and to approach the text and the author behind it in a manner that is active and engaged.

In keeping with the "I" and the "you" relation and the nature of this research as a kind of participation in meaning over time, I should give you some background on how I came to be involved in this work and these questions. As indicated in my preface, my concern with the experiential and educational implications of computer and Internet technology began with my engagement with these technologies in higher education in the late 1990s. As I helped to develop instructional Web sites at the University of Alberta and to support faculty use of WebCT, I was also learning about formal means of qualitative inquiry in the context of my doctoral studies in education. Although my readings, reflection, and observations became increasingly deliberate and systematic as my dissertation research began, there was no single, identifiable moment where my efforts stopped being informal everyday curiosity and turned into formalized inquiry.

I became engaged in a sustained and focused manner with the question central to this study around 2001. Between 2001 and the completion of this book, I have had much opportunity for observation and reflection, having taught in a variety of contexts, including graduate-level teaching at three institutions in Canada, and at a similar number of universities in Europe. Courses that I specifically taught online in these contexts provide me with recollections that are central to my descriptions and analyses in this book, with accounts of messages sent and received in these courses serving as the basis of my discussion of the relation between student and teacher. I have also drawn on recollections of my earlier work as a teacher's aide with mentally and physically challenged students in secondary educational contexts (occurring between 1992 and 1994). I have also drawn from reading in the literature related to the lived experiences of online education that has slowly been emerging with the popularity of the Internet.

Academic writing by other authors—especially ethnographic studies—has provided inspiration and, importantly, valuable experiential descriptions and descriptive material forms, and these are cited at a number of points in the book. Also, works of fiction (e.g., Brontë, Joyce, Salinger, and Calvino) have provided me with descriptions of the experiential dynamics of the relation between the schoolyard and classroom, student and teacher, reader and text.

Of course, I have also engaged in more formally and conventionally defined data gathering as a part of my research. During 2002 in particular, I undertook six in-depth interviews, with male and female research participants—both teachers and students—ranging from age 18 to age 45. These interviews were carried out as qualitative, hermeneutic interviews described above, sometimes in cafés and other times, in front of a computer screen, but always in a context with a minimum of structure and with a clear invitation to discuss striking incidents or recollections rather than evasive generalizations. In these interviews, I asked participants to recall relevant moments or incidents during their recent experiences in college or at the university. These interview sources have subsequently come to form the basis for some of the descriptive passages that are found at various points in this book. In cases when these passages have been taken from an existing, published, academic or fictional text, this source is of course cited as such. In cases where such a source is not cited, the descriptive passage emerged through the interviews or through experiential observation.

Each time a text like this book is encountered anew, it invites the reader to breathe his or her own life into its descriptions and meanings. It is in this way that a text can be corroborated or validated by new or returning readers. The possibilities afforded by this kind of writing and this book as a whole are ultimately and decidedly different from those based on objective measures or scientific tests. Thus, in addition to being invited to share the experiential evidence or meanings of this text, as the reader you are also requested to evaluate, to validate or invalidate these meanings, to agree or disagree with the interpretations presented about these moments of experiential significance and their interpretation. I also invite you, as readers and discussants, to reciprocate in the ethically charged "I - you" relation, and to help in closing the hermeneutic circle by contacting me directly with questions and comments via email at: nfriesen@tru.ca.

# CHAPTER 3

# The Peril and Promise of Language

IN CARRYING OUT A PHENOMENOLOGICAL INVESTIGATION OF the experience of the screen and the classroom, I have been paying special attention to language. As I showed in the previous chapter, language is constitutive of the life-world, of the realm of the intersubjective "we." In this sense, as Heidegger says, it is the "house" of our "being." At the same time, I also emphasized that language—as an element that is co-emergent with the life-world—brings with it a particular power and peril. It has the power to evoke and simulate experience, and it is perilous in that it can also sustain and reinforce what Husserl has called the "natural attitude." Language in this sense can disclose as well as cover up experiential aspects of a phenomenon, either unsettling or reinforcing aspects of our "liv[ing]-in-certainty-of-the-world." Just as it can make some experiences seem certain, mundane and inevitable, language can also evoke experience in ways that stir up emotion and sometimes even wonder.

The power and peril of language seems to be even more critical where computer and Internet technologies are concerned. These have long had a fraught relationship with language. For example, writing just after the advent of the personal computer, John Barry (1991) argues that "computer language" amounts to little more than "technobabble." It is characterized, he says, "*by anthropomorphic language*, excessive use of the passive voice, flash-in-the-pan neologisms, solecisms, synecdoche, euphemism, obfuscation, and mangled metaphors, among other traits" (p. 89). The language of the computer, in other words, appears as little more than a jumble of deceptive rhetoric. David

Thorburn (2003) argues more recently that similar properties pertain to the Internet and the Web. "The World Wide Web is more than technology, more than modems, bandwidth, computers. It is a thing made of language and of history." It is, in short, "a Web of Metaphor" (p. 19). Thorburn goes on to look at the specific metaphors of the "frontier" and the "open highway" as examples. In doing so, he uncovers some significant contradictions:

> computer users and web surfers navigate or manoeuvre across (or down or through) a superhighway, a teeming marketplace, a frontier, the vasty deep of cyberspace—yet all the while situated physically in safe domestic or professional cubicles, tethered to the computer screen... (p. 20)

The language of open frontiers and adventure belies the often banal conditions under which the Web is literally or actually used. These metaphors emphasize freedom, movement, and action, while ignoring or obscuring the physical confinement, immobility, and inaction associated with the embodied use of computers. This inconsistency, Thorburn argues, has the effect of distorting the experience of computer engagement, and preventing new and fruitful understandings of these technologies:

> we view all new technologies through perspectives or metaphors that limit our understanding and obscure intrinsic qualities and possibilities... So, too, though more dangerously, the dominant metaphors deployed to describe our experience of things digital constrain our understanding, limit and channel our inventions and even our speculations. (p. 19)

The question that I consider in this chapter, then, is how common terms and metaphors might similarly limit and distort some aspects of our experience and understanding of online and offline education—while simultaneously giving undue emphasis to others. I address this question by looking at the vocabulary used in discussing computer technology, the Internet, and education generally. Through this examination, I demonstrate how language achieves different types of distortion and disclosure in three specific ways:

1. Individual words can be used to bring together and confuse or conflate phenomena that are experientially very different, highlighting particular aspects of these experiences at the expense

of others. This is particularly common when a term used to identify or describe something offline is applied metaphorically to an online context or experience. I have already indicated that something of this kind occurs with words like "classroom," "class," and "seminar," which are used without differentiation both online and offline. In this chapter, I show how this is the case with the words "chat," "discussion," "student," and "teacher."

2. Words used in similar ways in both online and offline contexts can distort aspects of experience in both contexts. In many cases, these terms are reinforced by specific circumstances of online use, with their effects registered both online and offline. I show how this scenario is the case with the terms *user* and *use* online, and with the terms *learning* and *learner* in discourses on education in general.

3. A particular conceptual construct or theory can give to terms specialized but powerful meanings and associations, changing their definitions and possible uses in ways that are subtle but significant. I argue that this is the case with the "vocabulary" of learning and learners identified in point two, above, and the frameworks of psychological or "learning" theories associated with it.

It is clear that language can cover up distort and affect experience in many ways. In fact, no matter how carefully chosen and combined, all words take us away, to a greater or lesser extent, from some aspects of the experience. Even though language co-emerges with experience in life-world contexts, it subsequently has the power to "name" experience with greater or lesser resonance, and to bring us close to or pull us away from the immediacy of that experience. What is important is whether language does this very directly and overtly, or whether it is able to sustain some proximity to the experience in question. Based on consideration of a number of terms in this light, I outline a vocabulary that gives preference to some terms I believe are closer to or less closed off from experience than others.

After examining ways that language can overtly obscure and distort, I spend the final half of the chapter showing how language can also point to or reveal experience. An important part of the promise that language brings with it is the ability to "say more" than initially intended. Above all, through

metaphor, it has the power to carry implications and connotations whose significance can extend well beyond literal or face-value meanings. I show how
the multiple and complex implications of an important sequence of metaphors used in describing common educational technologies contain what van
Manen (2002) has referred to as the "phenomenological surplus" of language.

> *Words often mean more than they mean.... [S]ometimes the surplus meaning*
> *is phenomenological. It is phenomenological when the meaning is evocative of*
> *lived experience, when it re-awakens some possible human experience in a man-*
> *ner that is immediate and yet prompt[s] reflection. Thus language is a source*
> *of meaning; it makes our experience "recognizable." (n.p.)*

Metaphors and other figures of speech that are part of the language of online
education and educational technology, I believe, reveal important experiential aspects of education or pedagogy. Based on these experiential aspects,
I derive the outlines of a conception of pedagogy that is central to the later
chapters of this book. The intention of this chapter is thus to explore these
"extra" meanings and the power of language, but to begin by examining the
peril that it brings with it.

### The Perils of Generalized and Specialized Terms

The examples of "chatting" and "discussion" readily illustrate the nuanced
significance of words and metaphors in the language of online education.
Both terms are apparently straightforward and innocuous in their meaning, and designate specific parts of online educational environments such as
Blackboard or Moodle. In these systems, students and teachers are given the
option of engaging in a discussion or in a chat—often in addition to other
types of communication, such as integrated email or blogs. Technically
speaking, "discussion" (also designated by the terms "computer conferencing" or "bulletin board") refers to "asynchronous, text-based communications" that are "threaded" or otherwise systematically organized. Discussions
of this kind occur through the exchange of textual messages, which are
organized by their topic and the time they are sent. These communications are said to be "asynchronous" because they take place over a period
of days, weeks, or even months, rather than occurring in "real time." These
asynchronous communications are seen as having significant potential for

teaching and learning, are described as being especially suited for "discipline and rigour in... thinking and communicating," and therefore also as ideal for fostering "higher-order cognitive learning" (Garrison, Anderson, & Archer, 2000, p. 90). As a result, forums specifically designed for this kind of rigorous thinking and communication have been given titles that clearly reflect these high expectations. They have been designated as systems for "computer supported collaborative learning" (Stahl & Hesse, 2006), as technologies for supporting "communities of inquiry" (Anderson, et al. 2001), or even as "environments for knowledge building" (Scardamalia & Bereiter, 2003). "Chat," texting, or instant messaging, on the other hand, refers to textual communications that occur in real time (or "synchronously") and that are organized chronologically. Technologies designed for this type of communication have not attracted the level of interest among educators and educational researchers as their asynchronous counterparts. The fact that they are often simply referred to as "chat rooms" or "chat windows"—rather than environments for "knowledge building," "communal inquiry," or "collaborative learning"—is reflective of this lower status.

Like metaphors of computer technologies more generally, use of terms like *discussion* and *chat* can distort experience or "constrain our understanding" and "limit and channel our reflections," to use Thorburn's phrases. One way to get at these distortions and limitations is to compare how "discussion" and "chat" are used online versus offline. Online, in Blackboard or Moodle, chat and discussion are differentiated as specific "functions" with requisite "tools" for their realization. Offline, the difference between chatting and discussion is more a matter of degree. We differentiate rather unsystematically between subjects deserving serious *discussion* (e.g., a student's plans for his or her future), and others as occasions for just a *chat* (e.g., his or her plans for the weekend). Reflecting this differentiation, *Webster's* dictionary (2010) defines "chatting" as "talk[ing] in an informal and familiar manner." It identifies discussion, on the other hand, as "a formal treatment of a topic" or as the "consideration of a question in open... debate." However, we do not speak of an actual room or place exclusively for "chatting" and another as reserved only for "discussion." Even stranger would be a space designed and reserved specifically for a task like "knowledge construction" or for a "community of inquiry." In the offline world, these kinds of activities take place in much more mundanely and vaguely designated "environments": the classroom, office, study hall, or even hallway. Although the names of these types of rooms or places give some indication of purpose and activity (e.g., the classroom as a place for a class, the study hall as a place for study, or the hallway for getting from one place to another), they do not designate these functions as narrowly as do the terms used online. In addition, there is no need or expectation—in shifting from one mode of communication to another—to leave one space and enter another when a chatty exchange of greetings, for example, gives way to a more serious debate. Despite the fact that the same words are used to designate "chat" and "discussion" both online and offline, the actual places for conversation in these two contexts are rather different. Online, these terms emphasize purpose, function, and categorization of communication in a way that is not emphasized offline in through words like meeting room, hallway, or office.

Philosopher of space Edward Casey notes the flexibility of the relationship between place and intended function in the offline world. He observes that "[p]laces are built not only for such obvious purposes as shelter or prestige or comfort" (2009, p. 121). Such built places, perhaps especially those associated with transition like hallways, elevators, or sidewalks, may "foster experiences that [can] appear purposeless at first glance" (2009, p. 122). These include apparently "purposeless" activities such as spontaneous gatherings, hallway conversations, and nods and greetings in passing. Casey notes that locations are intentionally built in non-prescriptive, open, and flexible ways in order to accommodate these improvised, apparently non-purposive activities and experiences: "Thus we discern the special character of indirection in built places, their nonstraightforward aspects and roundabout features [which] are much more commonly characteristic of built places than we might first imagine" (2009, p. 122). As we shall later see, these nonstraightforward, non-prescriptive characteristics of built places exist in close complementarity with the similarly non-purposive multiplicity of the human body. Like them, the body cannot be reduced to a single function or meaning, and it always exceeds or evades any one function or significance that may be applied to it.

A conspicuous foregrounding of function and categorization similar to that provided by chat versus discussion environments is also evident in the online use of terms like *students, teachers*, and *administrators*. This system arises specifically from the way that these terms are defined through particular roles, permissions, and functions in online educational systems. On the surface, these words (and others used to designate educational roles or identities) are used online in similar ways to their use offline: to identify different functions and responsibilities, and to associate them with particular people. However, the reality of their use, online and offline, is rather different. In Blackboard or Moodle (and in many other networked computer and software systems), the roles and responsibilities of the student and teacher (or end-user and administrator) are explicitly associated with individuals when they log on to the system. Unlike students, teachers, or administrators who are offline, the *functions* for these identities are assigned in a manner that is quite inflexible and is given explicit definition down to the finest detail. For example, a teacher is able on Blackboard or Moodle to give tests, delete messages, create content and assignments, and view all of the minutiae of students' activities in the course. An administrator in the same system is able to do all of these things and more: add, delete, and rename courses, and change the parameters for all courses at once, for example. The student, on the other hand, can do only a very limited subset of these activities: access content, take tests, and post to the forums set up by the teacher. Organizationally speaking, roles are defined according to their bureaucratic ideal, down to the most minute allowances and interdictions.

Offline, however, the functions associated with roles and identities are much less rigid and explicit. As is the case with chat and discussion, students can readily play a part in the creation of content, can conceal (or deliberately highlight) their activity in the course, and can even sometimes even switch roles with the teacher. Improvisation and variation can occur with relative ease, and people are not assigned functions with their username and password. Instead, they can shed (or maintain) aspects of their role or persona inside and outside of the classroom according to preference and circumstance. Just as the use of "chat" and "discussion" to designate online activities differentiates and thus foregrounds function, so too does the way that roles and responsibilities of students, teachers, and administrators are defined online. In both cases, exactly the same terms designate activities and entities that are quite different in experience and operation online and offline—with the result that important differences between online and offline experiences and operations are covered over.

Insofar as computer and online technology requires roles and functions to be predetermined down to the slightest detail, it can be said to "enframe," to set up and to order these identities and activities in the manner ascribed to technology in general by Heidegger. Whether it is recognized or not, "students" and "teachers" online, like "discussion" and "chat" in the same context designate much more specifically and explicitly their purpose or *function* than their offline counterparts. Function, or "the purpose for which something is designed" (*Random House Dictionary*, 2010), is essential to technology, and the fact that it is foregrounded by technology in general means it is central also for this study. Speaking generally of technology in terms of tools or "equipment," Martin Heidegger (1962) explains that "[e]quipment is essentially something 'in order to'" (p. 97). Technologies, in other words, are means designed in order to achieve ends. If this "in-order-to" or this means-ends structure is fundamental to technology, then it is possible to say that online is different from offline because its "equipmental," "technical" quality is more evident and unequivocal. The purpose, the function or the "in-order-to" of what is encountered on the Web, in other words, is more explicit, specific, and is presented with greater clarity and less ambiguity—even though it can be partially hidden by the use of undifferentiated or ambiguous language.

Perhaps a simpler way to make this argument—specifically as it relates to online communication—would be to say that people do not generally enjoy a moment or modality in online educational settings in which they just "show up."[1] They are generally not seen as being present but simply idle. Instead, people in online learning environments are designated in advance generically via functions or things they do, in terms of the deployment of course tools and the accessing of Web content. We are subtly but irrevocably enframed by the function of the tools, forums, roles, and permissions. Furthermore, we are confronted by a language that at the same time works to erase these differences, that repeatedly equates online and offline, tacitly

....................................................................................

1  Woody Allen has famously observed that "Eighty percent of success in life is just showing up" (as quoted in Levine, 2010).

but insistently making the case that our experience in both contexts is fundamentally the same.

## Users, Learners, Persons, and Students

Function is thus foregrounded by terms that designate different phenomena, online and offline, with great specificity but without explicitly differentiating between online and offline variations. Function can similarly be foregrounded by very general terms that designate a wide range of phenomena, both online and offline. However, they acquire much of their authority from online contexts. This is the case, I argue, for the words "use" and "learning" (and for terms related to them). Speaking of all ways of engaging with computer technology simply as use and labelling all ways of developing and acquiring knowledge and skill simply as learning, these terms have the effect of de-emphasizing factors separating different types of uses and different aspects of learning. What is highlighted in their place is a single element that has significant affinity with the online world: one of generalized function or instrumentality. Moreover, this element is emphasized in terms of what can be readily or habitually thought and put into words in connection with the words "use" and "learning." A comparable idea has already come up in my discussion of experience as "information" or "data" that are received, processed, and that subsequently form the basis for what we know and think. All of the different characteristics of experience, its emotional hues, its spatial, temporal, embodied, and relational dimensions are covered by a single category: "information." Indeed, this simplification helps set the parameters for how questions and challenges of experience and communication are posed and framed—specifically as problems of information and its transmission.

The terms *use* and *user* cover a wide range of possibilities, experiences, and dispositions, and end up being applicable to almost any way of employing or engaging with computer technology. For example, persons intensely involved in playing a game on a computer or composing an email online are not simply employing this technology like a tool such as a computer virus scanner or even a bottle opener. They can be said to be absorbed or immersed in their task and in the technology with which they are engaged. At other moments, those designated as "users" may simply be distracting themselves with the technology, languidly browsing the Web, playing solitaire, or shuffling icons around on the desktop, doing "nothing much" rather than "something in particular." To say that all of these ways of spending time in front of a computer screen are simply instances of "use" and that those engaged in them are "users" is to abstractly categorize a wide range of experience, to subsume forms of engagement that can be manifest in very different ways, under a single undifferentiated label.

To apply the term "use" to all of these instances, moreover, is to tacitly confirm that the computer is just a "tool"—something that is designed to be used—rather than something more multifaceted. Despite the broad generalization implied in the terms *use* and *user*, they have the effect in this sense of reducing the relationship between technology and person to one of function. The idea of employing a tool in order to accomplish a task is emphasized at the expense of other possibilities of absorption, distraction, engagement, or disassociation suggested above. As Andrew Feenberg explains, many critics of the computer and the Internet have characterized these technologies as profoundly "depersonalizing" and have argued that the language of use and users literally replaces the individuality of persons with generic, decontextualized functions:

> the computer reduces a full-blown person to a "user" in order to incorporate him or her into the network. Users are decontextualized in the sense that they are stripped of body and community in front of a terminal and positioned as detached technical subjects. (2004, p. 98)

Neither Feenberg nor I wish to dismiss the computer and the Internet as being actually as reductive as the language of use and user implies. My aim, instead, is to focus on the variety of experiential possibilities facilitated by computer technology, regardless of the reductive, uni-dimensional character suggested by the language of use.

The terms *learner* and *learning* (and related phrases like "learner community," "learning outcomes," and "learning environments," for example) present similar issues with similar implications. Even though the terms *student* and *teacher* (rather than *learner* and *learning facilitator*) are used as labels for specific roles and permissions in online systems like Blackboard and Moodle, the words learning and learner are broadly associated with new approaches to education, especially those enabled or supported by the Web and the Internet. Examples of phrases that combine "learning" or "learner" with reference to these new technologies (or their capabilities) are easy to find. They include Web-based learning, technology-supported learning, computer-based learning, computer supported collaborative learning, networked learning, online learning, blended learning, ubiquitous learning, open learning, flexible learning, distributed learning, and e-learning, to mention a few.

Like the issue of computer "use" and "users," these ways of using the word *learning* have been associated with controversy and critique. Referring to examples of new educational labels and programs, both online and offline, educational philosopher Gert Biesta criticizes what he calls the "new language of learning," and says that it has gradually taken the place of a rather different vocabulary defined in terms of "education":

> One of the most remarkable changes that has taken place in the theory and practice of education over the past two decades has been the rise of the concept of "learning" and the subsequent decline of the concept of "education." Teaching has become redefined as supporting or facilitating learning, just as education is now often described as providing learning opportunities or learning experiences. Pupils and students have become learners, and adult education has become adult learning. ...The idea [overall is] that education should be about meeting the predefined needs of the learner. (2006, pp. 15, 22)

What is of initial importance here is that the words *learner* and *learning*, like the terms *user* and *use*, cover the widest range of persons and activities. This designation could arguably not be any more general and all-encompassing; in theory, it excludes no one. It is difficult to say that someone at a given point in their lives is not experiencing and also learning something new, making every person a learner, and every activity a potential learning experience. At the same time, learning, like computer engagement, can have many different modalities, ranging from learning how to ski or navigate a new city, to learning the intricacies of calculus or the nuances of a foreign language. All of these types of learning, of course, are experientially distinct. Employing the terms learning and learner in each of these instances—like referencing the word "user" in relation with computer technology—covers over this heterogeneity, and highlights only one particular, common characteristic at the expense of all of the others.

As with the case of computer use and users, this single characteristic is about function. Speaking of users, use, learners, and learning foregrounds an instrumental relationship between the person "doing," the activity being "done," and the goal accomplished. Both suggest the "in order to" structure invoked by Heidegger: Just as a person who is a user is defined (implicitly) as using the computer like a tool to accomplish a specific task, "learner," as Biesta argues, is a person who is actively engaged in a process to acquire determinate knowledge or skills. When the vocabulary or "language" of learning is applied to other educational entities and phenomena, they are also arguably integrated into the logic of given means undertaken for identifiable ends. A school or classroom becomes a "learning environment," designed to facilitate the implementation of pedagogies or rather "learning theories" by a teacher or better, a "learning facilitator." This structure is adopted to maximize the accomplishment of specific "learning goals" or "outcomes." This way of speaking aligns each of the elements involved in education as a means to a predetermined and particular end: The teacher is supporting learning; the environments and techniques used are designed to accelerate learning, and this acquisition of knowledge is brought to a much finer, instrumental point in pre-determined "learning outcomes" that these accumulated means are intended to achieve.

### Interactions, Relationships, Environments, and Life-Worlds

The functional emphasis expressed through terms like *user* and *learner* is further reinforced by their connection to other terms and concepts in the context of larger theoretical frameworks or structures. These frameworks bring further implications to bear on these terms and to subtly alter the kinds of meaning they can and cannot be used to express. Of particular importance for this study is that in the case of the learner in particular, these frameworks clearly avoid reference to specifically experiential and human elements, and instead reference phenomena relevant, in theory, to nearly any kind of animal or life-form. Examples are provided by terms like *behavior, environment,* and *interaction* in phrases like "learner behavior," "learning environment," and "interactive learning." These types of words and phrases are not deficient in and of themselves. However, in their generality and widespread use, they subtly foreground that which is instinctual and unthinking at the expense of reflection and self-awareness.

Simply put, behavior, interaction, and environment are terms or concepts that are as relevant to pathogens as they are to persons: both can be said to "behave" in a particular manner, and to "interact" in specific ways with their respective "environments." In one case, this environment is a host body; in the other, it is a classroom or an online context of some kind. However, the same cannot be said of terms such as *comportment* and *habit* (instead of behavior), relationship or interrelation (instead of interaction), and "world" or the phenomenological term *life-world* (in place of environment). Terms like comportment, relationship, and life-world encourage consideration of at least some of the complexities implied in human sociality, self-awareness, and intentionality—complexities that are of no small importance in education. On the other hand, by virtue of their biological generality, terms like environment, interaction, and behavior can be said to subtly discourage consideration of these same complexities.

One way of further illustrating these distinctions is offered by Hans-Georg Gadamer, who differentiates between life-world and environment by appealing to his understandings of language and experience, as described above. The "environment," Gadamer explains, designates surroundings that are separate from language, that are "wordless to begin with" (2004, p. 417), whereas humans are always oriented to the life-world through language:

> *To have a world means to have an orientation* (Verhalten) *toward it… This capacity is at once to have a world and to have language. The concept of world is thus opposed to the concept of environment, which all living beings in the world possess… In a broad sense… this concept [of environment] can be used to comprehend all the conditions on which a living creature depends. But it is thus clear that man, unlike all other living creatures,[2] has a "world," for other creatures*

2   The assertion that all non-human creatures are without a "world" in Gadamer's sense of the term has recently been contested. For example, the idea that primates can have different cultures and that their experience is thus ordered according to particular cultural norms has been gaining currency. I attempt to avoid the issue of the possibility or impossibility of animal experiential worlds in my discussion here. I do so by pointing out the applicability of terms like environment, interaction, and behavior to pathogens and other comparatively simple life forms that are more clearly excluded from culturally mediated experiences and meanings.

*do not in the same sense have a relationship to the world, but are, as it were, embedded in their environment. To rise above the pressures of what impinges on us from the world means to have language and to have "world." (pp. 440–441)*

We have and share a life-world, in other words, through language. In co-emerging with experience, language furnishes us with a context, a background for our abilities, plans, and actions that is always already replete with meaning.

The use of terms like *environment* and "*behavior*" are also connected with specific frameworks or theories of development and education that have fairly explicit and revealing intellectual histories. Ways of defining learning in terms of a human's (or an organism's) behavior in a certain situation or environment can be traced back over one hundred years in the history of psychology. Around the turn of the century, Edward Thorndike and other behavioral psychologists began to conceptualize human education and development by looking at how animals modify their behavior in response to environmental conditions or stimuli. In fact, psychology as a whole was defined by Thorndike as "the science of the intellects, characters and behavior of animals including man" (1910, p. 5). Speaking specifically of schooling, Thorndike further asserted that "any problem of education" can be reduced to a single, simple question: "Given a certain desired change in a man, what situation shall we create to produce it, either directly or by the response which it provokes from him?" (1912, pp. 55–56). How, in other words, can an environment be manipulated to produce positive changes or learning in the human or other organism in that environment? As behaviorism gave way to cognitivism, and cognitivism to constructivism, the specific learning theories used to frame and address the "problems of education" changed—but the centrality of a functionalist vocabulary of learning, interaction, and environment remained. Cognitivism saw learning in terms of environmental inputs of data and of their efficient processing in the mind; constructivism replaced this interpretation with learning as the development and interaction of representations of the environment (and their improvement from naive to expert levels).

As I indicated earlier, the use of phrases such as learning environments or interactive learning is not wrong or erroneous in itself, but the prevalence of this vocabulary subtly directs attention away from specifically human concerns and toward frameworks of instrumentality and functionalism that could apply to a range of biological systems. Terms like *behavior, environment,* and *interaction,* in other words, can be said to be farther from human experience than words like disposition, world, and relationship. Through their association with human awareness and intentionality, words like relationship and world bring us closer to a range of characteristics of everyday experience, including relationships that carry significance and meaning, and the dispositions and even moods that shape our experience of the world around us.

Despite the fact this dynamic can be seen as a matter of emphasis and word choice, it is possible to argue that it is of central concern for many discussions of education. Unlike organisms in general, humans are aware of and are able to account for what they are doing rather than simply acting or behaving out of pre-programmed instinct. For example, we can do much more than interact: We can cultivate relationships and networks of relationships that have histories and nuances of meaning that are both shaped and expressed through language. We are expected to be responsive and responsible in such relationships. Our worlds are structured via the meanings provided by an accountable, intentional awareness, rather than strictly in terms of mute instinct. In fact, it is a central task of education to cultivate relationship, awareness, and explicit accounting of intentional purposes and decisions, rather than to direct innate patterns of behavior, to boost the efficiency of cognition, or to reshape naive into more "expert" constructions. In this sense, education and learning are similar to engagement with computers: They can take forms, like browsing and play that are not reducible to a single goal or a specifiable subset of objectives. Like these types of engagement, education and learning can, and surely sometimes should, be seen as less a means to an end than an end in itself. However, because of the instrumental orientation of the vocabularies of learning—subtly reinforced as they are by technological language and designs—education gets enframed as an activity that can be optimized to pre-determined ends, and in terms of specialized means allowing for greater or lesser efficiency and effect. It is conceived of, in short, as a technology.

I do not presume that I can simply "undo" all of the ways that we are "set up" through the technologies and the vocabularies that they bring with them. As I have said, these are vocabularies that sometimes hide the difference between online and offline contexts, while at the same time introducing a covert insistence on instrumental priorities as common to both. Of course, we cannot simply invent new words or categories to overcome the obfuscating and instrumentalizing effects of any and all terms. However, by putting these terms into question, and by recognizing the significant difference in the meaning of certain terms online and offline is a good place to start. In this study, I hope to undo (at least some of) the enframing functionalism of online technologies by using alternative words that avoid an unnecessarily overt emphasis on technological utility and that are not unnecessarily distant from the life-world and human experience. Thus, instead of speaking of a user's or learner's interaction in an online environment, I speak of a person's life-world engagements online. I use the more traditional terms of student (rather than learner), classroom or course (rather than learning environment), teacher, education, and pedagogy (rather than referring to separate means of facilitating learning). The student, unlike the learner, is historically, culturally, and institutionally contextualized, is therefore not readily subject to abstract and a-historical functional definition. The student is also capable of participating in multiple modalities of engagement, many of them not explicitly instrumental or reducible to a single goal. The teacher, generally speaking, is in the same position: He or she is granted a role that has social, cultural, personal, and other significance, and that is much broader than any particular expert function of "support" or "facilitation." Also, except when I am addressing issues specifically of functionalist tool use and usability, I speak of persons being "engaged with" the Web and the screen, and I seek to use more specific terms like *writing, reading,* or *browsing* in place of the generic term *use.* Of course, some terms such as *chat* and *discussion* cannot be replaced quite as easily; they designate online contexts and practices by force of convention, and the alternatives (e.g., speaking of forums for synchronous communication or for communal inquiry) may simply foreground specialized function even more explicitly. Thus, while I retain some conventional online vocabulary, I use these terms advisedly, recognizing the differences that in some cases separate their meaning, offline and online.

The purpose of working with terms in this way ultimately goes back to the framing of the question outlined in the first chapter. In formulating the question of the significance of the spaces of the screen and classroom for pedagogy, I described a number of important characteristics for such a question. Quoting Gadamer, I noted that what is essential for any question is that it "open up possibilities and keep them open" (2004, p. 299). Similarly, it is important that this study be open to the fact that computers and the Internet can accomplish a great deal as tools or technologies; at the same time, it is important to also keep open the possibility that they are much more than tools: They are places that facilitate some experiences while limiting others.

## The Power of Language: Phenomenological Surplus

Simple and innocuous words like "chat," "discussion," and "user" are significant because they foreground some important experiential aspects of technology (e.g., its enframing functionalism) while distorting others (e.g., qualitative differences separating online and offline). While this observation illustrates the peril of language, other metaphors and terms provide examples of its power. I explore some of these now by providing an overview of the figurative or metaphorical terminology that has been used to describe and promote computer and Internet technology in education over the last 50 years. In doing so, I identify a number of patterns in this history that can serve as positive attributes of education more generally. Patterns or consistencies in the way technology is described and promoted point to common experiences and expectations for education overall.

Like the language of computers and the Web generally, the vocabulary used to talk about computer and Internet technologies in education is highly figurative and metaphorical. Metaphor is defined as the substitution of one term or category on the basis of a similarity between the two. Proclaiming, for example, that "my love is a rose" or that "communication is information transmission" is to describe or define one thing in terms of another, in terms of the similarities apparent in each. The fragile beauty of the rose is substituted for one's beloved, and the transfer of data stands in for the activity of communication. In fact, some histories and overviews of educational technology organize the history of the field in terms of a succession of metaphors, in which computer technology is cast in a number of broadly metaphorical functions, roles or categories. The introductory textbook, *Computers in Education*, suggests, for example, that *all educational applications of computers can be placed into one of three major classifications: tutor, tool, or tutee. In this categorization scheme... the computer takes on three different roles. It serves either as a tutor (i.e., teacher), as a handy tool, or as a tutee, (i.e., student). (Merrill et al., 1996, p. 11; see also Taylor, 1980; Jonassen & Reeves, 1996; Taylor, 2003; Bull, 2009)*

In describing the computer in education as a tool, tutor, or tutee, it is the computer's function that is subjected to a process of figurative substitution. All of these terms are metaphors for the educational function of the computer. A number of authors have more recently argued that a fourth and final metaphorical association should be added to this sequence: namely, computer technology as a means of communication or as a medium (e.g., Bruckman & Bandlow, 2003). By briefly looking at all of these "metaphors" for computer technology, my point, though, is to provide much more than an historical and metaphorical overview of computers in education. I am attempting to get at some important aspects of pedagogical experience—the phenomenological surplus meaning identified by van Manen—that is hidden in these metaphorical designations.

The early use of computers in education was understood in terms of the significance or role of the computer as metaphorical tutor or teacher. This relationship is illustrated in early computer applications such as drill and practice or interactive exercises, which operated as follows:

*the computer acts as a tutor by performing a teaching role. In effect, the student is tutored by the computer. These types of applications are often referred to by several different labels such as computer-based instruction (CBI), computer-assisted instruction (CAI), or computer-assisted learning (CAL). The general process is as follows:*

1. *The computer presents some information.*
2. *The student is asked to respond to a question or problem related to the information.*
3. *The computer evaluates the student's response according to the specified criteria.*

*The computer determines what to do next on the basis of its evaluation of the response. (Merrill et al., 1996, p. 11)*

Such applications relied on expensive mainframe computers, which occupied a whole room, but could be shared by many students engaged in drill and practice simultaneously at separate terminals. Proponents of this approach set themselves the ambitious goal of tutoring 40,000 students simultaneously with a single mainframe computer and at a cost of merely 50 cents per student per hour (Szabo, 1992).

The second metaphor for understanding the significance of the computer in education, which developed with the rise of the personal computer in the 1980s, substitutes the computer with the term "tutee" or student. This approach is associated with Seymour Papert and his LOGO programming language. LOGO is a "simplified" or "friendly" language designed to allow students to formulate (among other things) "geometric commands... to draw objects" on a computer screen (Jonassen & Reeves, 1996, p. 699). The key is that by using this programming language to tell the computer what to do, the metaphorical roles of the student and computer could be reversed. Instead of the child merely being tutored, led, or "programmed" by the computer, with LOGO, it is the student or child who instructs the computer, in effect telling it what to do. Papert explains:

> In most contemporary educational situations... the computer is used to put children through their paces, to provide exercises of an appropriate level of difficulty, to provide feedback, and to dispense information. The computer [is] programming the child. In the LOGO environment the relationship is reversed. The child, even in preschool ages, is in control: The child programs the computer. And in teaching the computer how to think, children embark on an exploration of how they themselves think. (1980, p. 9)

The student is designated as a "tutor"; and the computer is metaphorically recast as a student or "tutee." Teaching subjects like math and geometry by programming the computer or "tutee" was at this stage seen as the best way of gaining a deep understanding of these subjects. Confident of the power of this new approach, Papert went so far as to predict the end of conventional schools and schooling themselves:

> I believe that the computer will allow us to so modify the learning environment outside the classroom that much if not all the knowledge that schools

*presently try to teach with such pain and expense and such limited success will be learned, as the child learns to talk, painlessly, successfully, and without organized instruction. This obviously implies that schools as we know them will have no place in the future. (1980, p. 19)*

As the personal computer became increasingly commonplace and its powers extended beyond number crunching and simple graphics to include animation, real-time manipulation, and rich multimedia, the dominant metaphor for explaining its educational value changed: Instead of being cast as a tutee, in need of instruction, the metaphor of the computer as a powerful educational tool has received more and more attention. More than just a single-purpose implement, however, the computer was understood as an endlessly pliable multi-purpose device; and it was also described as a tool with specifically cognitive properties. It was cast, in other words, as a kind of intellectual implement uniquely suited to support the cognitive tasks involved in learning. Starting in the 1980s and through the 1990s, the computer was described in education as a "cognitive technology" Pea (1985), a "cognitive tool" (Kozma, 1987; Jonassen & Reeves, 1996), or a "mindtool" (Lajoi, 2000; Jonassen, 2006):

*Cognitive tools...are computational devices that can support, guide, and extend the thinking processes of their users if the users are in control of the computers, rather than being controlled by the computers. ...Learners and technologies should be intellectual partners in the learning process, where cognitive responsibility for performing is distributed to the part of the partnership that performs it best... learners contribute what they do best and technologies contribute what they do best—the learner is in charge. (Jonassen, Peck, & Wilson, 1999, pp. 14, 13)*

The metaphor of a mental or cognitive tool works by ascribing to the computer rather remarkable powers—powers to operate effectively as a mind, or at least as a part of the mind. The implication is that as a cognitive technology, the computer could work more or less directly with the mind of the student, amplifying or even reorganizing it. These powers, in turn, facilitated further metaphorical associations, with the computer described in terms of an equal, a peer, or an intellectual partner in the student's cognitive labor.

Finally, the emphasis on the student being in charge in this relationship, using the computer only to do what it does best, further reinforces the instrumentality or tool-like character of the computer in this metaphorical construct.

Although the computer is still sometimes understood in light of the metaphor of the tool or "mindtool," a rather different metaphor for the educational value of digital technology has been gradually taking its place. With the rise of the Internet and Web as popular media in the 1990s, the computer and the Internet have been increasingly described as a medium. In this context, these technologies are understood as representing media that connect students with information and most importantly, with each other (some suggest the term "social mindtool," see: Nuutinen et al., 2009). As the term medium itself implies, computers and the Internet are seen as existing in the "middle" of the relationships formed between different individuals. Writing in 1993, Linda Harasim provides an early account of this understanding:

> The fusion of computers and telecommunications over the past twenty years has created a worldwide web of computer networks; these networks, initially established for transferring data, have been adopted by people who want to communicate with other people. Human communication has become the major use of computer networks and has transformed them into a social space where people connect with one another. Computer networks are not merely tools whereby we network, they have come to be experienced as places where we network. . . [They] enable people to socialize, work, and learn based on who they are rather than where they are located. People have more choice. (pp. 15, 22; original emphasis)

This idea of the computer as a medium, providing a metaphorical space or place where people around the world can connect, has received renewed attention with the recent advent of blogs, wikis, and other "social software" on the Internet. Reflecting a slightly different emphasis, Stephen Downes describes the rise of media like blogs and wikis in education as follows:

> Educators began to notice something different happening when they began to use tools like wikis and blogs in the classroom a couple of years ago. All

*of a sudden, instead of discussing pre-assigned topics with their classmates, students found themselves discussing a wide range of topics with peers world-wide.... In learning, these trends are manifest in what is sometimes called "learner-centered" or "student-centered" design. This is more than just adapting for different learning styles or allowing the user to change the font size and background color; it is the placing of the control of learning itself into the hands of the learner. ... [The learning context is no longer] a single application, but a collection of interoperating applications—an environment rather than a system. (Downes, 2005)*

Downes is, in effect, re-stating and updating Harasim's earlier metaphor of technology-as-medium. However, Downes is also making explicit how more recent Internet technologies allow students to go well beyond the classroom to include other contexts and communities. Echoing Papert's statement about the school's obsolescence, Downes concludes his description of these new technologies and practices by saying that they are leading decisively away from traditional institutions or "intermediaries" of information and learning: "the structures and organization that characterized life prior to the Internet are breaking down." Downes says: "Where intermediaries, such as public relations staff, journalists, or professors, are not needed, they are disregarded" (2005). Envisioning the educational value of digital technology through metaphors, it seems, does not stop at simply linking a vivid image to a new technical function. It often involves articulating bold visions of the future of education generally. These visions extend from imagining thousands of students being tutored simultaneously (at a cost of pennies a student) to imagining of the ultimate obsolescence of the school, its roles, and organizational structures.

### The Phenomenological "Surplus" in the Language of Educational Technology

Interpreting the educational value of the computer in terms of metaphors of tutor, tutee, tool, and medium reflects more than changes in educational technology and theory. As mentioned earlier, these metaphorical equations—and the passages in which they are found—can be a source rich in phenomenological "surplus meaning." This meaning can be said to reappear at or just below the surface—in the accounts above and in the literature more generally—like recognizable shapes or patterns in a complex weave of claims and ideas. The first of these is the theme of relationship and the associated issue of relational symmetry; and the second, the theme of place, and the related question of its particular character. The recurrence of relationship and place over decades of research literature suggests that they are important to education and the use of technology in it. In this book, I go beyond this concept: I make the case that they lie at the very heart of pedagogy and its technologies.

Consider first the issue of place: This theme or meaning is revealed most prominently in the metaphor of the computer as medium. In accounts describing the computer as a medium, these information technologies are characterized not merely as "tools whereby we network," but also as metaphorical locations that are "experienced as *places*" (Harasim, 1993, p. 15; original emphasis). They are also described as technological "environments" rather than mere "systems" (Downes, 2005), as spaces where people "socialize, work, and learn" (Harasim, 1993, p. 22), and where they are able to discuss "a wide range of topics with peers worldwide" (Downes, 2005).

These online places for networking and learning are positioned, either implicitly or explicitly, in opposition to their counterparts offline. Harasim and Downes both indicate that these online places or environments allow students to reach beyond the physical walls of the classroom, enabling them to communicate "based on who they are rather than where they are located" (Harasim, 1993, p. 22). The "choice" and "control" (Harasim, 1993, p. 22; Downes, 2005) that this new medium makes possible, in other words, allows or even compels students to leave the physical classroom and its confining walls behind. Papert, writing two decades earlier, is just as unequivocal: He envisions the impact of the "computer as tutee" as being so dramatic that "schools as we know them will have no place in the future" (1980, p. 9). The computer screen, Papert is saying, will ultimately supplant the school and the classroom as the locus of education. A similar opposition between the spaces of the screen and classroom can be detected in the discussion of the computer as tutor. In this case, it is the screen of the computer terminal and the power of the mainframe computer that threatens to supplant the classroom as the domain of the teacher and of conventional teaching practice. The argument is that the computer will render this domain obsolete by virtue of the computer's sheer efficiency and cost-effectiveness (reducing expenses of teaching or tutoring to a mere 50 cents per student per hour).

The theme of relationship and the related issue of symmetry appear in all of the descriptions provided above. Each contextualizes the educational value of computer and Internet technology by invoking different kinds of relationships. Educational applications of these technologies seem to be typically or perhaps ideally situated in the context of a close and sometimes one-on-one relationship, in which reciprocal roles are defined in terms of tutor and tutee, teacher and learner, learner and learner. The technology is either itself ascribed broadly human and personal characteristics or is seen as powerfully facilitating positive relationships by acting as a medium between those it connects. In the earliest passages, the computer is described as relating to the student by "performing a teaching role" (Merrill et al., 1996, p. 11); later, it is the student who teaches the computer "how [to] think" (Papert, 1980, p. 19). As the computer becomes more powerful, it shares with the student the work of learning in a "collaboration" or "partner-ship" (Jonassen, Peck, & Wilson, 1999, p. 13); and most recently, the com-puter is seen as creating a "place" or "environment" powerfully facilitating the development of relationships by "connect[ing] people with other people" (Harasim, 1993, p. 13). It is in the context of such relationships that these people are able to "socialize, work," engage with "peers worldwide," and most importantly, "learn" (Harasim, 1993, p. 22; Downes, 2005).

In each of the four metaphors for computer technology in education, the relationship between education and technology is also consistently described or qualified in terms of its symmetry or perhaps more accurately, its asymmetry. What is highlighted in these metaphors, in other words, is the question of who leads, has the upper hand, or is in control in a consistently "lopsided" relationship that is, in one way or another, constitutive of teach-ing, learning, or pedagogy. In addition, with only one notable exception, the student is always envisioned as being firmly "in control" or "in charge" in this relation. The exception, of course, is provided by the metaphor of the computer as tutor, in which the computer is seen as being in control, guid-ing the student through a sequence of questions and answers or stimuli and responses. This emphasis on relational (a)symmetry or on student control begins with Papert in the 1980s and extends without interruption through Downes's description of social software. Thus, Papert envisions the LOGO programming language as enabling the student to move from a relationship where he or she is supposedly being "controlled," "programmed," or "guided" by the computer to one in which he or she is able to "guide" or "control" it (Papert, 1980, p. 19). Jonassen, Peck, and Wilson (1999) similarly emphasize that it is the student who is ultimately placed "in charge" when the computer is used as a cognitive tool. Lastly, Harasim and Downes stress simply that through the use of the computer and Internet as media, "people" are given "more choice" (Harasim, 1993, p. 22) and that "the control of learning itself" is placed in "the hands of the learner" (Downes, 2005).

These emphases on relation, on who is in charge in this relationship, and where such a relationship should unfold, are all themes that emerge with remarkable insistence in the literature of educational technology. They can be said to represent a kind of "phenomenological surplus" in the language used in this literature—an excess of meaning that points to something significant occurring beneath the surface of these discussions. In this book, these "surplus themes" are of great importance. In the chapters that follow, I will be using these motifs as a starting point for developing what I refer to as a "phenomenological" or "experiential" pedagogy.[3] This is an understanding of teaching and learning that is fundamentally *relational*. Conventionally, the relationship proper to pedagogy has been one between teacher and student, but, as the examples considered above make clear, this type of relationship continues to be questioned and redefined where computers and the Internet are concerned (and in other contexts as well). Computers take over one of the roles in the relationship between student and teacher, or otherwise facilitate the development of pedagogically significant relationships. Also central to this understanding of pedagogy is a notion of location, space, or place germane for the development of such a relationship. Both of these

---

3    My discussion of an "experiential," "phenomenological," and "relational" pedagogy owes much to a similarly phenomenological and humanist approach to this subject that has been articulated in Germany from the late nineteenth century through to the present. German-language sources developing this type of pedagogy include Dilthey's (1971) *Schriften zur Pädagogik* and Nohl's *Die padagogische Bewegung in Deutschland und ihre Theorie*. There are also several English language texts introducing this approach to Anglo-American readers; see: Spiecker, 1984; van Manen, 1991, 2002; and Friesen & Saevi, 2010.

aspects of pedagogy will be developed further in the course of this book—as it explores the question of the significance of places and relationships for pedagogy, both online and off.

*section two*

ACTING IN WORLDS: ONLINE
AND OFFLINE

# CHAPTER 4

# Screen and Classroom: Time, Space, and Body

EXPERIENCE HAS ITS HOME IN THE LIFE-WORLD, IN THE INTER-subjective realm in which time, space, body, and relation are "lived." Language co-emerges with this life-world, and, as a result, single words or longer descriptions can provide a form of "experiential evidence," whose validity can be gauged through reader involvement, rather than through any objective measures. As I explained in chapter two, the intersubjective world thus evoked through language corresponds to the perspective of the first person plural or "we." The "we" perspective overcomes the extreme opposition of the objective (third-person) and subjective (first-person) perspectives, and provides the methodological starting point for this book's inquiry.

I undertake this inquiry by looking into two of the most general, basic, and perhaps most common experiential elements of classroom and screen: The "online" experience of sitting down to work in front of the computer, and of engaging with words, images, and other things on the screen. Offline, this scenario would correspond to the experience of being called to class, working on a lesson, and engaging with pen, ink, and paper. I begin with these examples of engagement with objects—pen, paper, screen—rather than with persons in order to start simply, and to move to more complex interpersonal engagements later. (Chapters six and seven present a sustained examination of encountering and engaging with others online.) The experiential descriptions used in this examination are taken from a range of sources: from a book-length philosophical study, from academic articles, and also from works of fiction. Focusing on two of the four life-world existentials—time and space—in interpreting this experience, it is possible to trace a path that leads from general experiences of screen and classroom to more complex experiential forms that may also be more peda-gogically revealing.

### The Computer: Time, Space, and Body

In a paper entitled, "The Embodied Computer/User," Deborah Lupton, a sociologist and prolific writer, begins by describing her daily routine:

> *When I turn my personal computer on, it makes a little sound. This little sound I sometimes playfully interpret as a cheerful 'Good morning' greeting, for the action of bringing my computer to life usually happens first thing in the morning, when I sit down at my desk, a cup of tea at my side, to begin the day's work. In conjunction with my cup of tea, the sound helps to prepare me emotionally and physically for the working day ahead, a day that will involve much tapping at the computer keyboard and staring into the pale blue face of the display monitor, when not... looking out the window in the search for inspiration. I am face-to-face with my computer for far longer than I look into any human face. (2000, p. 477)*

Many people—whether teachers, students, or sociologists—start their day in ways similar to Lupton's, and like Lupton, they often end up spending the majority of their time during the day face-to-face with the computer.

Reading Lupton's description in light of the life-world dimensions or existentials described earlier, what is perhaps most striking is the way that space, time, and body are structured by routine or habit. It is in terms of habit, for example, that Lupton organizes the work space around her: with the computer in front, she sets "a cup of tea at [her] side," and readies herself for a day spent staring into the monitor—with only the odd glance directed elsewhere (out of "the window in the search for inspiration"). All of these activities are clearly part of a routine for Lupton, part of the "working day" for which she is careful to prepare herself both "emotionally and physically." Time, too, is experienced according to routine: Lupton "usually" brings her computer "to life" first thing in the morning as an initial step to begin her day's work. The "little sound" that the computer routinely makes adds a further element of convention and even of comfort, reinforcing the customary sequence of her working day.

The dimensions of time and space are also both indirectly implied in Lupton's sententious observation that she is "face-to-face" with the computer screen "for far longer" than she looks "into any human face." Implicit in this statement is what one phenomenological researcher refers to a "relational strategy." This strategy involves both the body and the mind and refers to the adjustment and adaptation required of both in engaging with a particular technology. Using the example of the technology of a magnifying glass, Robert Rosenberger (2009) writes:

> To embody a technology, one... must comport one's body in a certain manner. I use the term relational strategy to refer to the particular configuration of bodily habits, intentions, and conceptions that make it possible for a person to take up a particular stable relation [with a given technology]. For example, for a person to use a magnifying glass to enlarge text on a page, she or he must possess a particular relational strategy for embodying the device... This relational strategy involves certain conceptions of the magnifying glass, and certain bodily comportments and habits regarding its operation. (p. 176; original emphasis)

Just as the use of a magnifying glass in enlarging text on a page involves a strategy of positioning and aligning the text, the lens and the eye, so too does computer engagement with a computer bring with it its own type of comportments, habits, and embodiment. The face of the reader/writer and that of the screen must meet or "interface" at a prescribed angle, almost as parallel planes. Additionally, to do anything more than reading or watching the screen, both hands must also be engaged, one on the keyboard and a second on the mouse.

The computer can be remarkably fixed and inflexible in some of its demands over the space and time of those engaged with it; and its demands have few experiential parallels in the world of print or face-to-face engagement: Even books and documents, or acts of handwriting allow for a variety of positions, relational strategies, bodily comportments, writing or reading in bed, in an office, or on a bus. However, many of these strategies or "interface" configurations that are not possible when at a keyboard and in front of a screen. Even in portable or hand-held incarnations, engagement with the computer that is both "hands-on" (with a keyboard or other interface) and "face-to-face" (with the screen) apparently remains indispensable.[1]

In addition to the question of an embodied relational strategy, the experience described by Lupton has further implications for the experiential dimension of the body. The title of her article describes the user specifically as "embodied" (The Embodied Computer/User), and one of Lupton's principal conclusions in the article is that the "culture" of the computer generally seeks nothing less than to "deny the human body" (p. 482):

> *A central utopian discourse around computer technology is the potential offered by computers for humans to escape the body... In computer culture, embodiment is often represented as an unfortunate barrier to interaction with the pleasures of computing... the body is often referred to as the "meat," the dead flesh that surrounds the active mind which constitutes the "authentic" self. (p. 479)*

These observations, although bold and sweeping, are not out of line with what other researchers and observers have said concerning computers and the body—including David Thorburn's description, cited above, of the computer as "tethering" its users to the keyboard and screen. Others, writing on the topics of "new media" or "virtuality" have used the word "imprisonment" to refer to the way that the computer confines its users to the screen, the mouse, keyboard, and other devices. In *The Virtual* (2003), Rob Shields, for example, explains that this technology "both liberates and incarcerates" (p. 11). Similarly, in *The Language of New Media* (2001), Lev Manovich

---

1    Some exceptions are presented by adaptive and speech recognition interfaces, many of which allow differently abled users to engage in a broad range of relational strategies with computer devices. Of course, new and changing technologies continue to vary (and often reinforce) "hands-on" and "face-to-screen" strategies of relation or engagement. Video games, which have recently attracted significant interest in educational technology research and development, reinforce the connection of player to screen, keeping the player's hands inseparable from a controller (albeit one rather different from mouse and keyboard). Even more recently, tablet computers with multi-touch interfaces present other possibilities: Although they still require a clear alignment of readers' and browsers' faces to the screen, they facilitate much more variation in the way this goal is achieved (e.g., when standing or recumbent). Also, while these devices free the hands from mouse and keyboard, they frequently require comparable types of input on-screen (and are sometimes reconfigured via accessories to conform to more familiar strategies of engagement).

speaks of these media as effecting an "imprisonment of the body" (p. 105). Physical maladies associated with extensive computer use provide a different kind of evidence for these charges of the "denial" or "imprisonment" at the hands of the computer. From "Blackberry-" or "gamers'-thumb," through "work-related upper limb disorder," to "carpal-tunnel syndrome," these maladies are known collectively as "repetitive strain" or "repetitive stress" injuries—highlighting the very "repetitive," habitualized nature of engagement with computer technology.

One significant historical precursor for the experience of the relational strategies represented by the fixed arrangement of desk, keyboard, and screen is provided by the technology of the typewriter. Writing in the *Phenomenology of Perception*, Merleau-Ponty provides a description of this experience, simultaneously situating it in a discussion of habitual and embodied "knowledge":

> It is possible to know how to type without being able to say where the letters which make the words are to be found on the banks of keys. To know how to type is not, then, to know the place of each letter among the keys, nor even to have acquired a conditioned reflex for each one, which is set in motion by the letter as it comes before our eye. If habit is neither a form of knowledge nor an involuntary action, what then is it? It is knowledge in the hands, which is forthcoming only when bodily effort is made, and cannot be formulated in detachment from that effort. The subject knows where the letters are on the typewriter as we know where one of our limbs is, through a knowledge bred of familiarity which does not give us a position in objective space.... When I sit at a typewriter, a motor space opens up beneath my hands, in which I am about to 'play' what I have read. (2002, pp. 166–167)

When we sit at a keyboard (and monitor), to paraphrase Merleau-Ponty, spaces of action and spaces of vision open up in front of our hands and eyes. This terrain is highly habitualized and is intricately subdivided in space and layered in time: Through hundreds of individual keystrokes and acts of scrolling, clicking, and dragging, this type of engagement can be said to represent a process of weaving and reinforcing a complex web of habit. Indeed, this web of habit, to take the analogy a step further, connects, reinforces, and explains more general matters of habit, for example, the routine of sitting in front of a computer, staring into the screen much longer than we might actually engage with and look into the eyes of another person.

## The Classroom: Time, Space, and Body

The experience of the classroom presents a locus of space and time that is also highly habitualized. Many novels and stories describing the experience of the classroom have been written over the past two centuries. Apparent in many of these is order or habit that is sometimes harshly enforced by an "indefatigable bell," as in Charlotte Brontë's *Jane Eyre* (1847), or by other similarly relentless signals and calls. This dynamic is evident also in the passage below, from James Joyce's *A Portrait of the Artist as a Young Man*, originally published in 1916. In describing the elementary school experience of its protagonist, Stephen Daedelus, it also begins with a routine signal or call:

> *A voice from far out on the playground cried:*
> *—All in!*
> *And other voices cried:*
> *—All in! All in!*
>
> *During the writing lesson he sat with his arms folded, listening to the slow scraping of the pens. Mr. Harford went to and fro making little signs in red pencil and sometimes sitting beside the boy to show him how to hold his pen. [Stephen] had tried to spell out the headline for himself though he knew already what it was for it was the last of the book.* ZEAL WITHOUT PRUDENCE IS LIKE A SHIP ADRIFT. *But the lines of the letters were like fine invisible threads and it was only by closing his right eye tight and staring out of the left eye that he could make out the full curves of the capital. (Joyce, 1916/1997, p. 37)*

Routine and order pervade the time and space of this classroom as clearly as they do Lupton's computer use: A call of "all in" brings the students into the classroom. At a predetermined time, students are taken from one clearly defined space (the playground) to another (the classroom). The space of the classroom, as Joyce later indicates, is one that is ordered in rows, overseen from the head by the teacher (Mr. Harford). Once at their places in the classroom, students are expected to engage in activity that is not altogether different from the focused tapping and gazing of Lupton's computer user or Merleau-Ponty's typist: The work of writing, in which students learn how to form letters and also how to hold their pens. The interface or relational strategy here—the visual and motor space that is opened up for the writing student—are constituted by page, pen, book, and desk.

The body in this description is foregrounded in a number of significant ways. The arrangement of page, pen, ink, and desk requires particular embodied comportment and even discipline: Students are required to sit still in their rows of desks and to apply themselves to the physical and intellectual task at hand. The reason that the protagonist views this earnest activity as a passive onlooker in the description above is because his glasses had been broken in the playground. It is also in this connection that the dimension of lived body becomes important: Stephen's experience here is of a person who is largely excluded from the space of the text and of writing because of a significant (albeit temporary) bodily handicap. He can only make out the most obvious letters or shapes when he squints.

This elementary classroom description reveals many aspects of experience that are in keeping with the order, routine, and even the corporeal "incarceration" associated with the computer. At least historically, the experience of classrooms has been associated with a regimentation of time, space, and the body that can at least be broadly compared to the rigid and inflexible structuring of computer technology. At the same time, though, Joyce's description may provide an inkling of other possibilities. One of these is presented by the reference to the teacher "going to and fro... sometimes sitting beside the boy to show him how to hold his pen." This engagement of teacher and student points to the possibility of a kind of flexibility and interpretive openness that is explored in more detail below.

Virtuality: Space, Time, and Body So far, I have used descriptions of the life-world from fiction (Joyce), philosophy (Merleau-Ponty), and an academic article (Lupton) as kinds of experiential life-world "snapshots." Below the level of plot and character, these short passages present moments that might otherwise escape notice when viewed from the perspective of common sense or what I referred to earlier as the "natural attitude." Although I have so far emphasized similarities between the classroom and the screen, the descriptions I have used also point to some important differences—specifically in

terms of the presence or absence of others in these highly routinized habitualized settings. Despite the fact that Lupton's and Joyce's descriptions present
experiential time and space that is highly structured, in the case of Lupton's
description, this experiential space and time are emphatically solitary. She is
alone with her thoughts at her computer; even if she were working on a text
originally drafted by another; she is literally working on her own: She does
not "tap at the keyboard" or "look out the window" together with someone
else. Stephen Daedelus, however, is with a teacher and with many others his
age; and his fellow students are writing together.

It is in Joyce's description of the teacher and Daedalus's peers that a
second difference between the spaces of the screen and the classroom enters
into view: As Stephen is "listening to the slow scraping of the pens," he
is also able to observe the teacher, going "to and fro making little signs in
red pencil and sometimes sitting beside the boy to show him how to hold
his pen." The teacher, here, is involved in multiple modes of engagement
with his students, sometimes apparently marking their writing work, and
at other times writing it together with them. The computer, by contrast, as
a physical artifact, does not readily allow for this flexible, "multi-modal,"
and "co-present" cooperation: It is not simply by chance that Lupton taps
on the keyboard and mouse and stares into the computer screen alone—
these interfaces are expressly designed to accommodate only one person at
a time. They are inherent to a device widely called the personal computer.
While such a computer can, of course, enable people to write and revise a
document collaboratively, this collaborative work occurs through tools that
are nonetheless designed for individual use, with the users sending and
receiving information over vast spaces, but all the while remaining physically "tethered" to the keyboard and the screen.

At the same time, the descriptions by both Lupton and Joyce make it
clear that there is a second way in which space, time, and even the body are
at work here. Although both descriptions focus attention on the external
circumstances of the keyboard and screen, or of the desk, pen, and paper,
they also make it clear that these circumstances serve as a means to a very
different experiential end. Clearly, the experience Lupton describes is not
simply about tapping on the keyboard and staring out of a window and
into a screen, nor is the activity occurring in Joyce's classroom simply about

"the slow scraping of the pens" on paper. Instead, in both cases, these activities are means through which another realm of experience and meaning are accessed. This realm is represented by the "virtual" world of the screen, which is accessed through the keyboard and mouse; it is also represented by the similarly abstract mental world of the text, accessed in the classroom through practices of reading and artifacts of ink and paper.

Each of these two virtual or abstract experiential "worlds" can be described in terms of its own dimensions of experienced time, space, and body. In the particular case of the computer, time is the real time of computation and information transmission, and alternatively, it can also be the "anytime" represented by the asynchronic dynamics of email or bulletin board exchanges. Space can be described in terms of the virtual cyberspace opened up and negotiated through the activities of navigating, browsing, or surfing. In the case of the printed text, this space and time are registered perhaps more subtly though the way we speak about immersing oneself in the "realm" of the text through acts of reading or writing. We speak, for example, of being "lost in a book" or as being otherwise caught up in the labors or pleasures of reading and writing.

To first examine the times and spaces of the Web and the computer, consider this experientially rich excerpt from "Tara's Phenomenology of *Web* Surfing"—an essay focusing on "liveliness" and the Web:

> *When I explore the Web, I follow the cursor, a tangible sign of presence implying movement. This motion structures a sense of liveness, of immediacy, of the now. I open up my "personalized" site at* MSNBC: *vital "instant" traffic maps (which the copy tells me, "agree within a minute or two real time"), synopses of "current" weather conditions, and individualized news bits, the Web site repeatedly foregrounds its currency, its timeliness, its relevance to me. A frequently changing tape scroll bar updates both headlines and stock quotes.... The numerous polls or surveys that dot* MSNBCS [sic] [Website] *promise that I can impact the news in an instant; I get the results right away, no need to wait for the 10 p.m. broadcast. Just click. Immediate gratification. Even the waiting of download time locks us in the present as a perpetually unfolding now.* (McPherson, 2006, p. 201)

The screen here presents a realm of experience that is tantamount to a life-world in and of itself. Its flat, glowing surface brings with it its own experiential dimensions of time, space, and body, in which the lived experience of "here" and "now" can be rendered plural and multiple while simultaneously being concentrated and condensed: There are various "heres" and "nows" presented by the constantly updated traffic maps and weather summaries, reporting on traffic conditions as they unfold on nearby roadways, and on developing weather conditions in Tara's part of the world and elsewhere. The constantly updated news and stock reports connect Tara's experiential present with that of disparate political and financial centers. The computer screen, in other words, allows us to be many places at once, to experience, in vicarious but multi-medial forms, simultaneous events in far away locations. There is also the "here" and the "now" of the cursor as it moves in "real time" across the space of the screen—and is followed by Tara as a "tangible sign" of her movement and "presence." The cursor, which can be rendered as an arrow and also as a hand, also is itself a "tangible" representation of the body's extension into this realm: like an embodied hand, it can point, reach, grasp, and move (click and drag, select, copy and paste), and can pick up and work with figurative tools, and otherwise handle, manipulate and engage.

Like the screen, the words of the printed page can also take the reader to far away times and places. However, these locales tend to be of a different nature: the page is static and linear in a way that is notably different from the multifarious or insistently active computer screen. These and other characteristics are highlighted in this cleverly self-reflexive passage about reading a book, written by Italian author Italo Calvino:

> You are about to begin reading Italo Calvino's new novel, If on a winter's night a traveler. Relax. Concentrate. Dispel every other thought. Let the world around you fade. Best to close the door; the TV is always on in the next room... Find the most comfortable position: seated, stretched out, curled up, or lying flat... Do it now, because once you're absorbed in reading there will be no budging you. (1982, p. 1)

Reading is characterized here as an activity that can properly take place only after the door is closed, the TV is left behind in another room, and other competition for attention in "the world around you" is otherwise allowed to "fade" away. This sequence of events is rather different from clicking on and navigating between the various widgets, tickers, and windows that can clutter a person's computer screen and simultaneously compete for attention. With such a screen before one, it would not seem incongruous to deal with even further competition and interruption, either onscreen or off: a streaming news broadcast, music playing in the background, or even a phone call would merely add one more element, one more vicarious, experiential "here" and "now" to the many that are already layered and offered for one's attention on the screen. Calvino's description, by way of contrast, demands that these competing elements be eliminated one-by-one, down to the level of distractions internal to the mind and body of the reader: "every other thought" should be dispelled; the reader is urged to "find the most comfortable position." The reason for this is because "once you are absorbed in reading," as Calvino warns, "there will be no budging you."[2]

In an exploration of the "phenomenology of space" in writing, van Manen and Adams (2009) describe how we must enter this "space apart" in order to "pass through... into the world opened up by the words, the space of the text":

> We have to make the physical space our own by positioning ourselves bodily, and mentally too, claiming a certain privacy. Then we have to claim a certain temporal space as well. We need an undisturbed space of time where we can dwell in the timelessness of the space of reading. (p. 5)

As van Manen, Adams, and Calvino all indicate, the body does not follow us into this timeless and non-physical space of the text. To provide access to the space of reading, the physical body should simply be brought to rest in a comfortable position in order not to bother the reader, who, after

---

2   Passages similar to Calvino's instructions concerning sensory deprivation and imaginary stimulation also appear in experiential descriptions of engagement with video games (and even horror movies). However, these gaming descriptions tend to focus on the cultivation of an atmosphere similar to that of the game, rather than on the issue of relinquishing the sensations of one world for another. For example: "Put in the game, turn the lights down, turn the surround sound up, pick up your rumble controller (please assure yourself that there are no young children peeking around the corner to watch), and you are truly ready to experience Dead Space...." (Royce, 2008); also: "As with the first part [of the game Decay], it's best to turn out the lights and maybe light a few candles in order to maximize the tension of investigating the dark corridors and condemned offices" (Wall, 2010).

all, "cannot be budged." At the same time, though, the life or experience of the body in the context of reading is not limited to the literal, physical body. There are other possible "corporeal" experiences. The text in which one may be absorbed, after all, has a corporeal existence, in the form of pages and text. Any document has its own "figurative" body (which, in some cases, can be further dissected into other body parts, such as a head[er], foot[er], spine, and even [dog] ears). Also, a text often describes the bodies, selfhood, actions, and feelings of others. In this sense it can also allow for vicarious experiences of embodiment. Correspondingly, the text can have an emotional effect on readers, sometimes even affecting them viscerally, bringing to life or to attention through the written word various experiential possibilities of lived body. Texts have been critiqued, bowdlerized, or even banned because their descriptions of the body were considered too emotionally affecting, disgusting, or revolting for their potential readership.

Just as the computer cursor and its many modalities "extends" the body onto the world of the screen, in reading, too, it is possible to experience embodiment in and through the text, both in terms of its physical form and the meanings that it can bring to life. In this sense, the lived body does not end at the skin or at the physical extremities. It is this experiential dilation or "extension" of the experienced body beyond the literal limits of its skin that emerges as an important theme in the next chapter, in which my examination of screen and classroom is extended into other educational spaces.

# CHAPTER 5

# Laboratory and Simulation: Intercorporeality

THE EXPERIENTIAL TIME AND SPACE OF THE COMPUTER screen and the classroom are manifold and complex. As shown in the previous chapter, screen and classroom incorporate two worlds:

1. the physical world of one's immediate surroundings, and
2. a "virtual," imaginary or mental world that is opened up by the screen or offered through the written page.

Of course, this opposition of classroom and paper, on the one hand, and of screen and digital media, on the other, is not absolute. Computers and digital media can, of course, be used in the classroom, and ink and paper are frequently used together with a computer outside of the classroom. Future development in technology and practice (e.g., laptops, e-readers, and blended learning) are likely to blur these boundaries further. In some senses, I present the opposition of printed text and computer screen for heuristic effect: to develop and contrast aspects of experience that are broadly associated with the "virtual" and the face-to-face in pedagogical contexts. As I indicated in the previous chapters, such a comparative exploration shows the world of the classroom to be characterized by an ambiguity and flexibility that is difficult to achieve through the explicit and pre-set functions of online spaces and software systems. At the same time, I also described how the distractions of the outside world are relatively easily integrated into the multiple times and spaces of the computer screen. They tend to be explicitly or systematically excluded, by contrast, in the experience of immersing oneself in a text.

In this chapter, I take this comparative exploration further. Instead of looking at engagement with text, I consider experiences associated with dissection, both in a virtual, online context, and in the physical setting of a school or biology lab. This examination reinforces some of the findings of the previous chapter: The physical setting of the school allows for a multiplicity of modes of engagement in the context of various instruments and tasks and the forms of engagement they elicit. The computer screen, on the other hand, offers a kind of engagement that is deliberately designed to be consistent and in some ways, circumscribed. In addition, it is precisely the question of the deliberate design of the virtual dissection—versus the "design" principles involved in a laboratory dissection—that lead to further significant and intricate differences.

## Dissection

The pedagogical practice of dissecting animals in school biology courses has long been associated with experiences, opinions, and debates of special intensity. Juliana Texley, an assistant school superintendent, observes:

> "I Remember Biology," parents often begin at their annual conference with the teacher. "That was when I dissected that terrible-smelling frog." The odor and distaste the dissection experience evokes have been among the most pervasive memories of secondary school science for more than a century. But in the 1990s, environmental consciousness, curricular concerns, and political pressure on schools have changed biology... (1992)

Some of the factors that have changed biology have developed out of important legal cases concerning in-school dissection. In the American context, one of the most prominent of these was heard by the California Supreme Court in 1987. It began with Jennifer Graham, a 15-year-old California girl who refused to participate in a school dissection on ethical grounds. When school officials refused to accept a project on amphibian behavior as an alternative, the young student took the school district to court. According to one report, "Graham became something of a celebrity, often called 'the frog girl,' who had the courage to stand up to the schools in her defense of defenseless animals" (Johnson, 1997). Today, in response to legal challenges and a number of other factors, schools and districts in the USA and Canada are much more sensitive to students' concerns and to other issues surrounding dissection. Serious consideration is now given to a variety of student concerns "rang[ing] from inhumane treatment of animals by the supply industry and the depletion of natural populations of affected species to concerns about the emotional responses of students who are 'turned off' to biology because of a dislike of dissection" (Haury, 1996, p. 2). Many schools and districts now recognize the legitimacy of individual students' wishes to opt out of dissections, with some institutions deliberately providing alternative assignments, and still others having dispensed with the activity altogether.

My aim in this chapter, of course, is not to focus on the range of complex legal and moral issues raised by dissection activities; it is instead to compare the experience of dissection as an online activity with its offline counterpart. In doing so, I pay special attention to the sensory and experiential intensity that has been associated with this activity—the fact that it has led to concerns with the "emotional responses of students" and that it remains vivid in the memories of parents with high school-age children of their own. Adapting the descriptive methods used in the previous chapter, I compare my own account of an online dissection with experiential data and passages gleaned from my own interviews and from a variety of research into in-school dissection.

## Body and Relation in Lab Dissection

Given its vivid and controversial nature, it is not surprising that there is a range of experientially rich accounts of dissection in both school and university science labs. Already, we have a kind of compressed experiential account in Texley's reference to parents' recollections of working with "that terrible-smelling frog." Accounts of classroom dissection typically follow a common sequence of events, punctuated by experiential moments of particular prominence that reappear with remarkable frequency.

One such moment is the experience of an initial encounter with or sighting of the animals to be dissected. Students typically notice them as they walk into the classroom, spotting "flattened rats in a jar" (interviewee), "little dead pigs lying in the sink," "a jar of pickled animals," or a creature simply "tossed... into a plate" (quoted in Solot & Arluke, 1997, p. 34). A second moment in the dissection that seems to stand out in even greater experiential relief is the act of touching and above all making the first incision into the dead animal or carcass. One ethnographic study of classroom dissection explains:

> The initial incision . . . the transforming cut and the only one made into a body that bears the obvious markers of "animal". . . is frequently the hardest one for students to make. Even some students who had never dissected predicted that "opening" the animal would be the hardest part. (Solot & Arluke, 1997, p. 35)

Whether the students make the incision themselves, or have others do it for them, their comments give special emphasis to the embodied and specifically visceral character of this moment. Here is one student's account in a study of the "high school dissection experience" involving a fetal pig:

> The first day, I thought I was just gonna be sick when Linda was actually slicing this pig open. I felt nauseated.... I don't handle blood and that kind of stuff very well. I was very glad that it didn't have blood in it. If it was a pig that had just died and had blood, I would not have been able to handle it....
> (Barr & Herzog, 2000, p. 64)

Interviewees describe the act of "touching a dead pickled rat" as "the grossest part" of the dissection, also saying that "first cut into" the animal, in which a liquid, presumably a preservative, "spurted" out, was particularly "gross."

The body in these cases is manifest experientially in a manner that is quite different from the embodiment associated with text, ink, and paper. Instead of being pushed to the background as merely one among many potential distractions from the task at hand, the body is very much in the foreground. It is, in effect, subject to a kind of sensual assault—one that extends from the sight of the animal to the sound and the tactile sense of the first incision. In addition, there are the smells of formaldehyde (which "refuse to leave your hands," as one interviewee says) and of rotting flesh (which was said to "get a little riper with each passing dissection session"). It also includes impressions and feelings of the "gut" as expressed through terms or phrases like "gross," becoming "sick" or "nauseous."

## Body and Relation in Online Dissection

A description of a virtual frog dissection provides a number of points of

FROGUTS INC. WWW.FROGUTS.COM

FIGURE 1: *Frog dissection*

clear contrast to the offline activities presented above:

*I log into my course web site, and click on a link called "Frog Dissection: try the demo at froguts.com"[1] as listed on the course outline. After waiting a few moments, I see an animated homepage that greets me with pleasant musical tones. I click on "demos" and then choose "frog" from a list. After another moment of waiting, an image of what appears to be a life-size bullfrog fills much of my browser window, with a row of buttons on the right. Underneath, text instructs me to "press the pin button on the toolbar" so that the frog can be secured. I do this, and a box of pins appears. I click and drag these pins one by one to spots on the frogs' arms and legs that are now marked with small red "Xs." I discover that I can then insert the pins simply by double-clicking. When they land in place, they make a dull percussive sound. Next, a red line running up and down the length of the frog's abdomen appears. I am instructed to "make 3 incisions along the dotted red line." I feel a slight sense of unease as I click on the button, and then drag a scalpel without resistance along the frog's glistening and mottled underbelly.*

This virtual scenario of dissection illuminates aspects of the lived body that, on the surface, bear greater similarity to Lupton's and McPherson's engagement with their computers than with students' engagement with the in-school dissection. Again, we see in the description a lived body that is extended onto the computer screen via "the cursor [as] a tangible sign of presence implying movement." Of course, this is not a real arrow, hand, or scalpel or pins, but a mobile and mutable signification of one's ability to engage in the simulation through actions of virtual manipulation, pointing, fastening, and cutting. The manifold sense impressions that assaulted the

......................................................................................

1   This diagram and the multipart description for froguts.com combine characteristics of two versions of the online dissection simulation: one version was openly available in 2002–2003, and a second "demo" version was accessed in the 2008–2009 school year.

body in the description of the in-school dissection are either absent or very much muted in this virtual activity: There is no smell of formaldehyde or rotting flesh; there is no need to fear that blood or any other liquid might come "spurting" from the creature being dissected. Moreover, instead of first seeing the animal "lying in the sink" or "flattened" in a box or jar, the first experience of the frog occurs while waiting for it to load in the browser window. Handling and even cutting into the animal, furthermore, is a question of clicking on the correct virtual instrument (the scalpel) and gliding it, in effect, across part of the computer screen.

Naturally, there is much more to a dissection than viscerally unpleasant and indelible sights, smells, and other sensations. There are well thought-out and articulated reasons for its inclusion in science and biology curricula—and these are stated clearly in school lesson plans and curricula. These reasons include ones like knowledge of "the structure and function of organs" (Jordan School District, 2004) and the safe selection and use of dissection "apparatus and materials" (Sackville High School, 2008). However, speaking experientially, impressions of disgust, nausea, and repulsion initially seem to overwhelm other, less visceral and more intellectual aspects of the in-school dissection. As mentioned above, this barrage of sense impressions is registered in the body in specifically visceral terms, in the stomach, in the form of feelings of nausea and sickness. The word "visceral" refers to the "the viscera or bowels regarded as the seat of emotion" (OED, 2007); a related term, frequently used in these descriptions, is "gross," meaning "plain, not delicate" or "uncleanly or repulsive in quality" (OED, 2007). In more formal accounts of in-school dissection, the term "squeamishness"—and its related meanings of nausea, sickness, queasiness, and disgust (OED, 2007) is repeatedly used to characterize student impressions of, and reactions to, dissection experiences (e.g., Barr & Herzog, 2000; Solot & Arluke, 1997). "Squeamishness" refers not only to a condition of the stomach, to the state of "being affected with nausea or qualms;" but it also corresponds to distinctly less visceral terms such as "disdainfulness," "reserve," or to "the quality... of being highly or excessively fastidious or dainty" (OED, 2007).

What is significant in these terms and definitions is clear evidence of a connection between the mind and the intellect, on the one hand, and the body and viscera, on the other. Defined in terms of "qualms," "reserve," or "fastidiousness," words such as gross, visceral, or squeamish can refer to an overwhelmingly embodied feeling, while at the same time, designating mental or intellectual state or position of defense, discomfort, or unease. A profoundly uncomfortable or disquieting situation or experience, in other words, can be experienced in terms of a deeply felt disgust or repulsion, and can simultaneously take the form of intellectual disquiet or moral qualms. Consider one undergraduate student's testimony in which he criticizes the ethics of dissection by recalling a particularly "sick feeling" that he associates not only with very visceral aspects of laboratory dissection, but also with less literally "visceral" events:

> I feel a sick feeling thinking about those labs. The same sick feeling I felt as a child when I saw a dead frog, shot by a neighbor kid in my creek.... The same sick feeling I felt when I found that [an old railroad landmark] in Tolono had been bulldozed. And the same sick feeling I felt when I saw a pedestrian struck and killed by a car in Phoenix . . . during a spring break trip. (Hassler, 2000)

The ethical implications of destroying a historical landmark, witnessing an accidental death, and dissecting a frog are obviously very different; but what is important in each case is the associated feeling of the lived body, and the students' reference to this recurrent feeling to justify an ethical and intellectual position against dissection. This approach further emphasizes the connection between embodied sensation and intellectual conviction, between feelings of the gut and impressions and decisions of the mind. In an article on the guts and learning, Robyn Barnacle (2009) observes the following about the viscera and knowledge:

> recognition of the emotionality of the gut is evident in everyday expressions, such as gutless, which refers to a lack of courage, or a fearful gut. In addition, both the notions of 'gut reaction' and 'gut instinct' treat the gut as a site of specific responsiveness to the world, the former in an immediate, unreflective sort of way, and the latter, conversely, as a particularly fine-tuned and insightful form of intelligence. (p. 26)

The gut provides us with ways of knowing that can be instant and immediate, but also subtle and insightful. For example, in the descriptions of dissection provided above, there is experiential evidence of a kind of communication, connection or relation between bodies: Cutting into the soft belly of an animal, or witnessing the injury or death of a pedestrian are illustrative of a kind of experiential relation that can exist between our body and those of others—even if those "others" are mammals or other kinds of creatures. Although these examples of incision and even death are extreme, this kind of connection and relation can be said to exist in more common-place and everyday contexts as well. This is a relation that is closely related to empathy, specifically as it is defined as the "project[ion of] one's personal-ity into (and so fully comprehending) the object of contemplation" (OED, 2007). This experiential aspect is the embodied or corporeal correlative to intersubjectivity it is discussed below using the term *intercorporeality*.

## Intercorporeality

The word *intercorporeal* is defined by Marjorie O'Loughlin in *Embodiment and Education* as a "carnal bond between human subjects, indicating that embodied subjects are connected in their 'belonging' to a common world" (2006, p. 135). The term is originally derived from notes in Merleau-Ponty's uncompleted text, *The Visible and Invisible*, where he uses the word "inter-corpor*eity*" to refer to "the sphere of life and the sphere of *Einfühlung*" (the German word for empathy; 1968, p. 172).

Like intersubjectivity, intercorporeality stresses the connection of ele-ments that are generally seen as being separate. However, we are no more entirely confined within the skin of our bodies than we are completely trapped in the subjective realm of our minds. Just as our subjectivities are melded in the intersubjective, so, too, are our bodies brought into a kind of mutual experiential contact through intercorporeality. This alignment is illustrated in students' responses to the incision of animal bodies in the class-room and on the screen, and also in terms of students' experiences of their own bodies—their feelings of nausea, sickness, or visceral unease. It is also manifest in terms of the existential dimension of lived relation—in the fact that this unease, discomfort, or nausea arise in the context of a relationship between bodies, in this case, the body of the students and the carcass of the dissected animal. Of course, this intercorporeal extension and connection between bodies does not always occur as strongly as is described above in the case of animal dissection. It can be experienced in terms of one person's or somebody's inviting warmth or another's defensive distance.

In keeping with Merleau-Ponty's reference to empathy, Marjorie O'Loughlin describes intercorporeality further as a bond between bodies that is principally empathic in character. She goes so far as to say that "living" itself "is about empathizing through intercorporeality" (p. 131):

> perceiving subjects are not confined within their own private worlds but are implaced within a world (made up of a myriad of sites) which is shared by all, no matter what their differences... Merleau-Ponty's articulation of a notion of intercorporeality provides an enlarged view of all human being, including those practices which we label thinking, knowing and judgment. (2006, p. 135)

O'Loughlin makes it clear that intercorporeality is an embodied connection between human beings that is an important, constitutive part of the shared, intersubjective life-world. It is expressed not only through feelings such as belonging, but also is a part of intellectual practices, which encompass judgment and knowledge, and also learning itself.

At the close of the previous chapter, I stressed that the phenomenological, lived body does not end at the skin. Instead, it extends far beyond this literal but arbitrary boundary into the space of the computer screen and the printed text. It also extends beyond its physical limitations through its engagement with other figurative bodies, such as the "body" of the text. It is precisely this extension or dilation that illustrates what O'Loughlin means when she speaks of an "enlarged view of all human being" (p. 135).

## Distantiation, Care, and Risk

As the dissection progresses, it moves from an initial and explicitly intercorporeal encounter with the body of the animal and its tactile and olfactory characteristics and becomes an exploration of its internal anatomy and physiology. Through this transition, a different set of experiential elements emerge. At the same time, the experience of intercorporeality, as an empathic connection between bodies in the dissection experience remains an important aspect but becomes more implicit in nature. One student interviewed for this study explains:

> The rat that we were dissecting had its tongue jammed out of its mouth and had clumps of fur sticking out everywhere; it kind of looked like Bill the Cat from the cartoon "Bloom County." So my lab partner and I named it "Bill the

Rat." *The fact that the rat looked like a cartoon character made the dissection easier to deal with.*

Similar techniques of distantiation, de-humanization or "de-animalization" (Solot & Arluke, 1997, p. 35) are apparent other accounts. For example, Barr and Herzog report that some "students cover[ed] the face of the animals they were dissecting," with one of these students explaining:

> *Every time we've worked on it (the pig) the face was covered. I couldn't cut the face. I could watch, and once the face was cut it didn't look like a pig anymore, and I could deal with that because it looked like—you know—a scientific experiment to me.* (2000, p. 59)

In the place of a strong intercorporeal link between the dissected animal and the student doing the dissection, a different relationship between the two is gradually emerging. Instead of being marked by a visceral, acutely empathic response, concerns of an intellectual nature come to the fore:

> *As these changes take place, the viewer's gaze is directed toward the newly exposed organs. One student observed, "You opened it up and the pig just like flapped down. You didn't see [the animal] when you looked at it. You didn't see the pig, you just saw like insides."... One student, who expressed ambivalence about the prospect of dissecting, said, "I couldn't physically open it myself ... but once it's open then I can look." (Solot & Arluke, 1997, p. 35)*

Although the smell of formaldehyde and rotting flesh certainly remain, they no longer combine with the sight of the animal's body to simply repulse students, making them squeamish, or "grossing them out." Instead, a different set of sentiments and impressions becomes possible. These include feelings of curiosity, a desire to explore and experiment, or in some cases, the emotional response of outright fascination. As one interviewee puts it, a kind of "conflict developed" for her "between the intricacy of the internal organs of the rat on the one hand, and its stinking and revolting body on the other." This interviewee also describes what was revealed in the rat's insides as a kind of "marvel: all of these little body parts, fitting and working neatly together like a sort of beautiful wet machine." Barr and Herzog say they "heard comments like "God, his liver is like a mushroom or something. His heart's kinda tough. Feel that," and "look at that. Ooh, it's got a weird texture" (2000, p. 63). Reflecting a more playful curiosity—or simply greater bravado—Barr and Herzog also report:

> On one occasion… boys in a group cut out their pig's intestines and stretched them almost completely across the room, inadvertently demonstrating the extraordinary length of the viscera to the rest of the class. (2000, p. 61)

A pig's small intestines, it should be noted, form a tiny ball together with the large intestines, but when they are uncoiled they can stretch to 20 feet or more in length. Whether the act of uncoiling this organ across the length of a room is judged in bad taste or as a legitimate experiment, it is certainly an act—like the exploration of an organ's tactile character—that has no direct equivalent in an online dissection. It is also worth noting that this kind of activity brings with it a special kind of risk, since it may not be entirely neat or tidy and is not reversible if done in error. As one student reports, "the rat got kind of mutilated," and sometimes the "organ or part that the instructor would point out would no longer be there."

The online dissection provides a similar emphasis on the work of accessing and exploring the deceased animal's viscera, but at the same time it provides many points of contrast.

> After the incisions are completed on the belly of the frog, a pair of scissors appears, and I am asked to "cut upwards with the scissors through the muscle tissue." I click on the scissors a few times, cutting along the tissue. But half way up the belly, text pops up advising me to "twist the scissors to avoid cutting the heart under the ribs." To do so, I click on yet another icon, and the scissors slip over to one side before I can continue cutting.
>
> Clicking and dragging through a few more steps, I am gradually able to see the internal organs of the

FIGURE 2: *Incising with scissors*

*frog. I am slightly surprised as my cursor turns into a magnifying glass, and I am able to zoom in on the animal's abdomen. A label appears for each organ as the magnifying glass passes over it. As I click on each of the labels, the organ's name is added to a list in a small notebook that has now appeared on the right side of the simulation window. I am rather amazed at how simple and seamless this all is.*

Emotions and impressions ranging from amazement to surprise are manifest in the simulated dissection, as they were in the descriptions of classroom dissection. Their significance, though, is rather different. In the simulated dissection, what appears as surprising and amazing is the responsiveness of the interface, the ease and convenience with which the dissection steps can be negotiated: one instrument replaces another almost magically, and they function together seamlessly. The student glides and clicks on the mouse as one dissection instrument is automatically replaced by another, and as labels hover over the dissected animal's body—to be recorded in the notepad with a simple mouse-click. Significantly, unlike the earlier description of the relational strategy involved in working with a magnifying glass (provided by Rosenberger in the previous chapter), working with and switching between the magnifying glass, the writing pad, and various dissection instruments does not involve a change in disposition or mode of operation. There is no particular "relational strategy" that might involve "bodily comportments and habits regarding [any one instrument's] operation" to quote Rosenberger. Instead, dissection is exclusively associated with those abilities, dispositions and habits that are part of using a computer. These skills have no more obvious relation to the activity of dissection than they do to any other activity that can be undertaken with the computer. In addition, for someone who has mastered the computer's generic interface skills, the online dissection may not be qualitatively different from many other tasks performed on the computer screen.

The emotions and responses in the classroom dissection (ranging from amazement to outright revulsion) are different from those of the simulation—in terms of their power, if not also in terms of their fundamental nature. These emotions arise not from the responsiveness and seamlessness of the activity. Instead, they are inspired, for example, by the appearance of the animal before it is dissected, or by the intricacy of its organs well after the initial incision has taken place. These emotions, whether negative or positive, are not inspired by the artifice of any designer, but arise from the natural or organic origin of the specimen at hand, for example, by the way that its internal organs are "folded" together, like a "beautiful wet machine." The difficulty and displeasure initially associated with the in-school dissection, as well as the intricate surprises that it may ultimately reveal, are all inseparably linked to the natural rather than artificial origin of the object involved.

Corresponding to the different origins of the simulated and "real" objects dissected is a particular type of "care" or attention that each elicits. The online exercise instructs the student to take care to turn the scissors onto their side "to avoid cutting the heart under the ribs." However, this particular instance of being "careful" and attentive involves a mere mouse-click. As far as the computer software is concerned, no one mouse click or keyboard stroke is necessarily more gently or skillfully executed than any other. Further reducing the need for care or caution is the fact that the simulation provides "back" or "undo" buttons or commands, allowing any one action to be immediately reversed. In fact, with the online dissection, there ultimately seems to be no chance of making an error with an incision or with any other part of the dissection activity in general. Taking care to avoid these types of errors becomes a matter of clicking and dragging in the ways and in the places as the simulation allows and instructs.

In the classroom dissection, irreversible errors, of course, can be made, and things can go wrong. As mentioned earlier, parts of the dissected body can be cut or removed in error, rendering further steps in the dissection process impossible to perform. There are other aspects of the dissection that require special care: The razor-sharp scalpel can do damage to living, human flesh as easily as it can slice the body of the dissected animal. Moreover, gloves and goggles must be worn to protect students' hands and eyes from formaldehyde and other chemicals, which are also deadly poisons. Different acts of incision, probing, and exploration, moreover, require different instruments and forms of dexterity and facility. One act of incision or act of probing can indeed be very different from another, in terms of its quality, its effectiveness, and its care. In addition, there is no way to simply undo a particular action or decision: In keeping with its natural origins, the body of the rat, pig, or other animal cannot be the subject of any sort of "undo" command—or be "refreshed," "reset," or "rebooted."

## The Virtual Dissection: Pliable, Discontinuous, Brilliant

The experiential possibilities and limitations presented by simulated and in-school dissections can be further explored by looking specifically at what it means for a concept or action to be virtual as opposed to being physical or real. Using terms like "virtual," "hyperreal," and "micro-world," theorists of technology have enumerated and described the qualities of these online, digital objects and settings. For example, Rob Shields (in *The Virtual*, 2003) describes how virtual objects and spaces

> have an elusive quality which comes from their status as being both nowhere and yet present via [technology]. . . . they also have duration but strictly speaking, neither history, nor a future. Of course there is a history of virtual spaces and of the technologies that make [them] possible. . . But inside a virtual space itself, there is only the immediacy of the scenario displayed. (p. 51)

Virtual objects, in other words, are not worn out or used up; they are not abandoned to decompose in a landfill. Unlike the formaldehyde-soaked carcass of a dissected animal, virtual objects do not have to be disposed of once they have outlived their usefulness. They can be repeatedly minimized, closed, reopened, and refreshed. In this sense, these virtual objects can be said to occupy a kind of placeless space and to inhabit a kind of timeless present or "immediacy," as Shields says.

Augustin Araya (1997) uses the phrase *microworld objects* to describe other properties of these virtual items and spaces. He characterizes simulated objects as lacking "certain kinds of functional and physical properties; for example," he says, "they cannot malfunction nor break in the sense that real objects do." Although they can freeze up or disappear from the screen, they generally cannot be "broken" or "mutilated" in ways that go beyond the preconceived limitations imposed by their designers. In the online dissection, for example, the student is simply not allowed to cut or explore the frog carcass in the wrong way. The only type of malfunction or breakage that can occur is instead of a completely different kind: the simulation can freeze up, or the browser or the operating system can crash.

In a critique of "hyperreality," philosopher Albert Borgmann characterizes virtual contexts and objects as being (among other things) "pliable," "brilliant," and "discontinuous and disposable" (1992, pp. 87–102). Borgmann describes hyperreal objects as being pliable specifically in the sense that they can be "entirely subject[ed] to…desire and manipulation" (p. 88). This pliability is perhaps most vividly illustrated in the descriptions of the online dissection in terms of the ease with which the virtual frog can first be sliced open, its organs revealed, then inspected with a magnifying glass, and finally noted with virtual pencil and paper. As mentioned earlier, no one tool or task in these activities requires a particular relational strategy or disposition that would differ from any other. For all of these steps or tasks, only relatively repetitive movements of the computer mouse are needed.

Borgmann describes the discontinuous and disposable characteristics of hyperreal objects and environments specifically in terms of their relationship to place, space, or context:

> To be disposable, hyperreality must be experientially discontinuous with its context. If it were deeply rooted in its setting, it would take a laborious and protracted effort to deracinate and replace it. Reality encumbers and confines. (pp. 95–96)

The account of classroom dissection above is rife with examples of encumbrance and confinement: This description begins with the persistent odor that is a part of the preserved animal's "context" (one that cannot be easily washed from one's hands), and extends to the irreversible incisions that might render certain organs absent or unidentifiable. Neither the process nor the product of physical dissection lends itself to discontinuity or disposability in the sense that Borgmann associates with the hyperreal: the toxic remains of the dissection are also all too persistent and present particular challenges for safety, cleansing, and disposal.[2] By way of contrast, undo and redo options or buttons on the virtual dissection are not so much

---

2   At the same time, it is important to note that the animal in this dissection has itself been deracinated or uprooted from its original context. However, for this radical de-contextualizing to have been successful, a laborious and protracted effort is required: the animal's body has to be drained of its natural fluids, and these have to be replaced with preservatives; the body needs to be kept in a sealed container, and once the dissection has begun, further steps need to be taken for its preservation.

convenient features as they are intrinsic properties for this virtual world—a world in which an object can be refreshed, rebooted, or simply shut down at will.

Borgmann describes the "hyperreal" quality of brilliance, finally, in terms of an "absence of noise" and a heightening of an object's "attractive" features. The "truly brilliant reality," Borgmann says, "would exclude all unwanted information" (p. 97) resulting in an experience in which only those aspects of explicit relevance are provided. In the online dissection, all (or nearly all) encumbering physical and intercorporeal aspects of the activity are removed; what remains is indeed "brilliant" in Borgmann's sense, from the textual prompts and dotted lines (that appear at precisely the times and places required) to the appearance and disappearance of instruments, labels, and other visual cues.

## Educational Brilliance

Borgmann's description of the brilliance of the hyperreal—and the systematic exclusion of all forms of encumbrance and confinement—is remarkably consistent with how virtual simulations are conceptualized in the literature of instruction and design. According to this literature, the tasks and activities to be modeled in a simulation are to be analyzed and enumerated according to how they might contribute to the attainment of specific educational objectives or learning outcomes. Those parts of the task or activity relevant to the educational objectives are retained or even heightened in the design. Those elements that are deemed irrelevant or unnecessarily confining and encumbering are simply excluded. Such a selection of elements is considered as a part of "instructional design," a field that works to "design…learning experiences" (Dede, Whitehouse, & Brown-L'Bahy, 2002) so as to maximize their instructional effectiveness and efficiency. Practitioners in this field sometimes reference a quasi-mathematical formula that captures the processes of inclusion and exclusion specifically for the design of simulations. For example, Jacobs and Dempsey (1993) explain:

> The supposition we make is that one only needs to simulate those events or characteristics that allow the learner to perform in a proficient manner when

*performing in the operational environment, i.e., the real world. This represen-*
*tation of the characteristics of simulation have been characterized by Gagné*
*(1962), and later by Clariana in the following formula:*

*Simulation = (Reality) – (Task irrelevant elements).*

*(p. 200; see also Smith & Ragan, 1993, p. 65; Leemkuil et al., 2003,*
*p. 93; Chandra & Sharma, 2004, p. 106)*

A simulation, in other words, is a representation of the "reality" of a task or
activity, with only those elements included that are required for the attainment of predetermined learning outcomes, or predefined measures of learner
proficiency. All other elements and components of the designed "experience" would be subtracted or eliminated in order to maximize instructional
efficiency.

As indicated earlier, educational outcomes typically associated with
dissection include "knowledge of [the animal's] internal anatomy," "skills
and processes [for working with] primary data" (Scholl, 2007, p. 2) and
the "practice [and] understand[ing of] dissection [as] a method of scientific
investigation" (Mondragon, 2005, p. 4). It is precisely by eliminating elements that do not explicitly or directly contribute to the attainment of these
goals—and by including and heightening these elements that do—that the
online dissection simulation is designed. Its design and operation instantiates this inclusion and exclusion in a way that is very deliberate, rigorous,
and systematic. Using Borgmann's terms, it excludes any "noise" that would
"encumber" and "confine"—from the persistence of the animal's body to the
insistence of the smells emanating from it. And it includes those features—
such as labels, pins, scissors, and a magnifying glass—only when their presence is instructionally and practically desirable. The end product, then, is as
"pliable" and accommodating of Borgmann's notions of "discontinuity" and
"disposability" as possible; it is as fully deracinated from any environment,
laboratory or otherwise, as its design will allow. In short, the simulation can
be said to be "brilliant" in a way that is specifically instructional or educational. However, does this way of conceptualizing design completely capture
and exhaust the pedagogical significance or value of the activity—whether
virtual or real?

## Dissection: Interface, Encumbrance, or Upheaval?

To begin to answer this last question, it is necessary to reflect specifically on the different origins of the objects or bodies being dissected. A virtual object, for its part, typically develops, or rather, is developed on the computer screen through the actions and interactions of instructional, technical, and graphical designers, and other experts. In this process, as already indicated, all aspects of the simulation are developed and coordinated according to specific, enumerated, instructional objectives. The original development of the organic object dissected in the lab, of course, occurs very differently, taking place through "natural" processes of (re)generation rather than through artificial acts of production. It does not occur in a workplace or on a computer screen, but in the warm and wet darkness of a body. This body can be the body of the animal itself, or the womb of its mother. This development, in other words, occurs through a kind of propagation and differentiation of elements of flesh and bone—through processes of gradual folding and unfolding, shaping and reshaping of proliferating, living matter. Of course, this process does not revolve around explicit, educational objectives, but occurs for reasons (if they can be called that) which are rather different. To summarize simply, the virtual object is designed by someone for explicit human (educational) purposes, whereas its physical counterpart develops on its own for purposes that are (at best) implicit and are not directly reducible to human ends.

As a piece of software developed by experts for explicit, human ends, the simulation exercise differs in other ways from the in-school dissection. Like any other piece of software, students engage with the simulation via an interface. The interface provides the means by which the various components and tools of the simulation are accessed and manipulated. A quick look at the language used in the literature of interface design reveals some interesting patterns related to phenomenology—a kind of phenomenological "surplus meaning." This vocabulary for interfaces includes words such as "seamlessness," "transparency," "translucency," "playability," "learnability," "flow," and "intuitiveness" —all of which designate desirable design attributes for interfaces (e.g., see: Usabilityfirst, 2010). This vocabulary makes it clear that one of the goals of interface design is a kind of comfortable certainty and familiarity. Moreover, this type of experience is clearly resonant with the kinds of terms Husserl uses to describe intentionality. Intentionality, as discussed above (see chapter two), refers to the everyday purposes, plans, and categories that connect us with the world around. It renders the world familiar, enabling us, as Husserl says, to "live in certainty of the world," and in this sense sustain the everyday, commonsensical "natural attitude." Terms such as seamlessness, transparency, and intuitiveness all suggest that the person engaged with an interface or a computer (whether working or playing) should be able to become familiar with its features and functions in a manner that is easy or "intuitive." The smooth operation of and inter-action with the interface is thus rendered relatively clear or "translucent." Furthermore, the interface is then also able to provide a virtual domain in which an individual is able to operate in an uninterrupted, intentionally directed "flow," a flow that is said to represent a deliberately maximized or "optimal experience" (Csikszentmihalyi, 1990). Computers, and particularly their interfaces, are designed to anticipate and facilitate what we want to do, when we want to do it. In the dissection exercise, as a very simple example, scissors appear precisely when an incision is required, and a magnifying glass takes their place when closer inspection is needed. This smoothly flow-ing motion from one tool to another is intended to provide students with an experience of uninterrupted transparency and flow, and a sustained but pre-reflective assurance of "living-in-certainty-of-the-world."

Simulations and interfaces achieve this approximation of Husserl's natu-ral attitude by hiding the myriad complexities and overcoming the many discontinuities that exist in any sophisticated hardware and software system. The simulation is designed, for example, to be compatible with the broad-est range of browser software. The student's attention thus does not need to be interrupted by considerations of the varieties of browser software, or the history of their development. The simulation—like any other computer interface—is designed in such a way that the student experiences minimal disruption, despite the complexities and discontinuities that may underlie it. In this state of "seamless" engagement or even "flow," what the student does encounter, though, is a manifestation of the world of human intentional-ity: means directed to meet human (i.e., educational) ends, all constructed for certainty and familiarity—and all carefully avoiding any unnecessary encumbrance or discontinuity. As a result, in engaging with a simulation, a student can be said to encounter (and also expect) something akin to her own intentionally structured world. In this realm, the students' own intentions—taking up the "natural attitude" and "living in certainty of the world" —are to constantly be served and reinforced. Students accustomed to computer technology thus encounter a set of tools that is quite familiar and pliable because it has already been integrated into their understanding of who they are and their understanding of their place and purpose in the world around them. In this sense, one could suggest that in engaging with a virtual world, students, in some substantial way, encounter themselves.

During the lab or in-school dissection, by contrast, the student is confronted with an activity that is neither familiar nor comfortable, neither convenient nor accommodating. It is part of an experience of the visceral or corporeal that is out of the ordinary, and that cannot be readily and completely reduced to everyday intentionality, plans, and actions. On a physical and practical level, the body of the animal in the classroom dissection encumbers and confines, requiring the student to use different tools and techniques to access, differentiate, and manipulate it at various stages in the activity. Each tool (magnifying glass, scalpel, probe, and so forth) brings with it its own relational strategy; a different embodied and conceptual comportment or disposition. The animal body did not develop or emerge through processes of design and testing in order to optimize the experience of a "user"; it is not encountered through an "interface" that is supposed to fade into transparency to allow the student to achieve goals as easily and conveniently as possible. The nature and arrangement of each of its organs, moreover, can be said to be expressive of specific goals and purposes, but these are not the goals and purposes that are not educational, human, or that we generally deal with as intentional beings—they are a part of a world that is generally hidden from us and clearly separate from our "living-in-certainty-of-the-world."[3]

If the simulated dissection confronts students with aspects of themselves—of the intentional ordering and certainties of the world around them—then the classroom dissection can be described as a context in which

....................................................................................

3    As one phenomenological study (Leder, 1990) shows, the world of our own internal organs is generally experienced in either a manner that is shadowy and indirect, that is experienced more directly only in very extreme, life threatening situations (e.g., an operation or critical injury).

students encounter that which is not the self, which is radically "other." In this "other," students encounter that which is unfamiliar, non-conforming and alien to their everyday purposes and plans as intentional beings. The radical "other," according to phenomenologist Bernard Waldenfels, is manifest as a kind of disruption of the self, its world, its plans, and intentions. Waldenfels goes so far as to describe the manifestation of the other as an "upheaval," and he adds: "As far as such upheavals are concerned, one can only yield to them or withdraw from them" (2007, p. 30). One could say that this choice between yielding and withdrawing captures the situation faced by the students in the in-school dissection exercise. The purpose of drawing distinctions between the virtual and the "real" in this way is not to enter the fray of arguments directly for or against animal dissection. Instead, I am attempting to broaden the factors or criteria considered in such arguments—and to link them to the nature of pedagogy and pedagogical experience. Like all experience, pedagogical experience is about an encounter between the self and the world. This experience can have the character of an upheaval or disruption, or it can be planned and optimized in advance, down to the finest detail. Both of these types of experience—experiences of inconvenience, encumbrance, disruption or of familiarity, pliability, flow, and brilliance—are important in education. For example, the attribute of "brilliance" that Borgmann ascribes to the hyperreal can be seen as being of significant pedagogical value (as the above reference to "educational brilliance" already suggests): The elimination of irrelevance or noise, and the foregrounding of that which is relevant or important is, with good reason, an indispensable part of lesson planning and instructional design processes. In many contexts, "educational brilliance"—and the associated phenomena of flow, transparency, and learnability—makes sense as educational goals. However, we should not conclude from this argument that such experiences represent the sum total of what is desirable for education. We should also not conclude that technologies designed to facilitate this type of brilliance and flow can be easily adapted to very different kinds of experience.

This last point is illustrated by attempts to simulate experiences associated with encumbrance and inconvenience. A specific example of this virtual inconvenience is provided by the warning in the frog dissection simulation to carefully "twist the scissors to avoid cutting the heart under the ribs." What the simulation actually requires at this point is a mouse-click that is no different—no more "careful" or skillful—than any other. To simulate this type of care, and the encumbrance and confinement that it presupposes, is to work against the very logic, design, and purposes of the computer and its interfaces. Attempts to simulate encumbrance, confinement, and other experiences like deprivation or deprival,[4] end up being experienced as either trivial or futile. They are seen as arbitrary or unnecessary irritations, rather than as challenges inherent to the task itself. If a more significant disruption takes place in the online dissection—a browser or operating system crash, for example—such an "upheaval" would not be proper to or draw attention to the dissection exercise itself. It would instead draw the student's attention to the computer or the simulation software itself, and perhaps also to the artificial nature of the simulation as well. The relationship between the self and the world, and the encounter of self and other is central not only to experience, but to pedagogy as it is understood in this book. The next chapter resumes this analysis by focusing on the encounter between the self and the human other in the classroom and in the context of online discussion.

---

4    An example of other experiences difficult (if not impossible) to simulate is provided in Marc Prensky's essay on "Digital Natives, Digital Immigrants." In it, he encourages the development of simulations for all types of curricula, even for subjects as problematic as the Holocaust: "Create a simulation where students role-play the meeting at Wannsee, or one where they can experience the true horror of the camps" (2001, p. 6), he suggests. The inability of simulations to render deprivation, encumbrance and confinement—along with experiences of risk and care—would clearly standing in the way of approximate the "true horror" of the camps.

*section three*

ENCOUNTERING THE OTHER ONLINE
AND OFFLINE

# CHAPTER 6

# The Body and Relational Pedagogy

AFTER SETTING UP THIS BOOK'S QUESTION AND METHOD OF inquiry, I have so far shown how the life-world that the computer presents has its own, manifold, experiential times and spaces. I have examined these times and spaces in terms of encounters with objects (texts and other information sources) and with other bodies (specifically in the context of animal dissection). I have shown how objects and bodies encountered in the online life-world possess particular qualities all their own. When compared to their counterparts in the "real" world, virtual artifacts manifest a pliability, brilliance, discontinuity, and disposability that can have educational value. At the same time, the virtual worlds of the computer present certain limitations that prevent some types of experiences, such as encumbrance and disruption—and the risk and care that they might entail—from being adequately simulated or represented. I also showed that these types of experiences are part of an encounter with that which is different from the self, or that which is "other"—and that the experiences of seamlessness, transparency or flow that the computer seeks to sustain are more closely associated with the self and the structures of its intentionality.

Still, in examining this question of self and other, I have not yet considered the experience of the human other, of social relation. The intersubjective, intercorporeal life-world is a reality that is collectively and socially constituted, and it comes into full existence only insofar as we share it with others and encounter and engage with others in it. My principal task in this chapter and in much of the remainder of the book, therefore, is to examine and reflect on this human and relational aspect of the life-world—to delve into the question of relating to others or more abstractly, the question of "otherness" or alterity. The real or simulated body of the rat, frog, or pig fetus can be said to have represent a kind of "quasi-other" (e.g., see Irwin, 2005)—an entity that is perceived as being (or having been) capable of entering into a kind of relation with the self. As was the case with the "otherness" of the body of the pig, rat, or frog, our relation to the "other"—whether animal or human—is a profoundly ethical matter: In the act of dissecting a real or virtual animal body, and in any other engagements with alterity, questions of right and wrong, responsibility and irresponsibility emerge as paramount.

When we engage with other humans, we say "you," and we are in turn addressed as "you." The "second person-" or "you-perspective," as discussed in chapter two, is itself all about ethical knowledge and engagement. One of the key characteristics of this ethical engagement is its reciprocity and mutuality. The fact that I say "you" and am in turn addressed as "you" suggests that my experience is echoed in that of others, and that a potential echoing of address, and a corresponding echoing of awareness and perception is constitutive of the relational dimension. Consonant with his understandings of intercorporeality and empathy, Merleau-Ponty (1968) uses the term "reversibility" to characterize the "idea that every perception is doubled with a counter-perception" (p. 264). According to Merleau-Ponty, all forms of perception—from vision to touch and taste—follow a self-reinforcing circular course between self and other, and between self and the world around it: "There is a circle of the touched and the touching, the touched takes hold of the touching; there is a circle of the visible and the seeing, the seeing is not without visible existence…" (1968, p. 143).

The act of seeing the other implies that the self, too, can also be seen; and the act of touching similarly implies the other's experience of being touched and his or her potential to reach out and touch. In these and many other ways, we share an experiential world through our bodies, perceptions, words, and actions, and in a manner that is both mutual and reciprocal. This experiential reciprocity presents at once both possibilities and limitations for understanding the other. For the reciprocal or mutual character of experience is by no means direct or absolute; aspects of one's experience, actions, and expressions may remain unknown and unknowable to others. This dynamic makes the ethical character of the relationship between self and other inherently problematic and continuously challenging: Despite the fact that we are bound together intercorporeally and intersubjectively, we remain in other ways separate, unknown, and unknowable.

## The Tone of Meeting

The passage provided below is the first of four interconnected descriptive accounts that are included in this chapter and in the next. It presents an introductory message sent by an instructor to a Web-based discussion forum at the very start of an online course.

*[Forum: Week 1 Discussion]*

*Article No. 1: posted by Gilles Simon on Sun, Oct. 5, 2008, 07:34 Subject: Welcome!*

*Hello, all*

*It's a crisp, fresh October morning here in Edmonton as I write this message. The ground is covered with golden and brown leaves, and I can see the steam rising from the river through the window of my second-floor study. Inside it is nice and warm. It is a similar, comfortable warmth that I hope to extend to you through this message. I want to welcome you all to the first week in our course, and to our humble discussion forum!*

*Let me first tell you a little about myself: I've been an instructor in Distance Education for five years; I have a Master's Degree in Education, and am currently working on my PhD. I've taught this course a number of times before, and every time I teach it, I learn more about the subject matter from my students. So I'm looking forward to learning more about the readings and also about who you are—and to engage in productive work and discussion with you on the topics in this course.*

*For our first assignment, I am asking you to reply to this message. Please introduce yourself as I've just done, telling everyone a little about your academic and technological background and interests, and also about your main aspirations or goals for this course. (Note that you can do this anytime over the coming week.) In this way, I'm hoping we can all begin to develop a fruitful and supportive online community. I'm looking forward to getting to know all of you!*

*Warmest regards,*
*Gilles*

In this message, the instructor is doing a good deal to try to set a particular tone or atmosphere for the course that he is teaching. As in the case of the descriptions of Per and Ari (see chapter one), the tone here is unmistakably positive, affirmative, and supportive. It communicates in its own way a measure of the warmth expressed in for example Per's comfortable but "particular humorous glance." The author of the posting, Gilles, says he wishes to extend to his students a "comfortable warmth..." and he tries to evoke this warmth by depicting his own personal situation: For example, by describing "the crisp, fresh October morning" that he is able to see from the comfort of his second-floor study. In addition, Gilles goes beyond simply stating his hopes and wishes for openness; he actually demonstrates or performs such openness by being relatively frank and unguarded in introducing himself, in characterizing his educational background, and in expressing his own desire to learn through the discussion.

All of the instructor's descriptions, explanations, and instructions are clearly in keeping with the guidelines and recommendations outlined in books and articles devoted to the subject of the "moderation" of online discussions. For example, one article providing "guidelines for moderating online educational computer conferences" explains:

> *The first thing a student will read when entering an area of the conference should be a welcome message written by the moderator. Online, as well as in person, first impressions are critical and once made, cannot be reversed. The welcome message sets the intellectual tone of the conference and must be carefully written to present the proper impression. If crafted well, the message can create a good deal of the appropriate atmosphere. (Winograd, 2003, p. 54)*

The author compares the composition of effective online welcome message to the act of making a good "first impression... in person." In both cases, such an impression is indispensable in creating an "appropriate atmosphere" or "intellectual tone." At the same time, though, Winograd's description shows that there are significant differences between online and face-to-face situations in the specific way that a good first impression is achieved. The welcome message, he emphasizes, must be "carefully written" and "crafted well" in order "to present the proper impression." Online, there is a clear emphasis on qualities such as "craft," skill, and on the "careful" exercise of one's compositional abilities. Having myself worked as an instructor in a number of online courses, I have eventually come to use a kind of standard "Welcome message" not dissimilar to the example provided above. I initially composed it with great care, taking a significant amount of time to draft, read, revise, and double-check it. Each time I send it out to begin a course, I improve and modify it slightly to fit the particularities of the course and the students.

In face-to-face situations, the cultivation of an appropriate atmosphere occurs rather differently. Instead of involving the careful and deliberate exercise of descriptive and compositional skill in front of a computer screen (over what can be an extended period of time), this cultivation of tone or atmosphere entails much more spontaneity and much less direct control. Tone is not set through the work of descriptive evocation, careful wording, or even a description of one's own background. Instead, a kind of tone can be expressed or "set" through what might be called a person's attitude, disposition, or even their "presence" in the classroom. The initial encounter with students is not a matter of a specialized or explicitly taught skill or ability, such as the ability to write. Instead, it arises through a combination of aspects or qualities, for which teachers generally receive no particular training or instruction. This unteachable, "non-specialized" repertoire of traits includes general attributes such as posture, gesture, facial expression, and tone of voice, but can also be traced to more specific characteristics, such as a glance of the eye, or a set of characteristic habits or gestures. As an illustration, it is worth remembering Per's "particular humorous glance," the way he says "yes?" after "a tiny little pause" and also the way he "leans back comfortably and waits." It is these embodied and perhaps even unconscious actions that are an inextricable part of setting an affirmative tone or atmosphere that is valued by the special needs student described earlier. In the remainder of this section, I will focus on issues of tone and atmosphere, looking specifically at how these issues are discussed in terms of online and face-to-face settings.

In his discussion of "telespectatorship" and "telepresence"— the idea of being remotely "present" through video, audio, and even robotics—phenomenologist Hubert Dreyfus discusses something similar to classroom experience by using the term "mood." Dreyfus raises the question of whether or not mood is fundamentally dependent on physical presence, and he speculates that it would be "lost" if someone engaged in social interaction via telepresence:

> *Ask yourself, if you were a telespectator at a party, would you be able to share the mood? Whereas, if you are present at a party, it is hard to resist sharing the elation or depression of the occasion. Likewise, there is always some shared mood in the classroom and it determines what matters—what is experienced as exciting or boring, salient or marginal, relevant or irrelevant. The right mood keeps students involved by giving them a sense of what is important.* (Dreyfus, 2008, p. 59; original emphasis)

One can easily imagine of Dreyfus's telespectator wishing to be present if the occasion (at the party or in the classroom) is warm and positive, or being glad to stay at a distance should it have a negative or depressing mood or atmosphere. It is important to note that the sensibilities and abilities that are a part of this kind of contextual atmosphere entail a special emphasis on the *personal* rather than the professional. Gilles's opening account of his background specifically as a *student*, and the description of his immediate surroundings in his home office can be seen as an attempt to initiate a specifically *personal* relation with the students in his course: it is a distinctly *personal* warmth—one "relating to… a person as a private individual" (OED)—that he invokes and says he wishes to extend to everyone in the class at the beginning of his messages. And he ends the message by saying, *I'm looking forward to getting to know all of you!*—indicating, in effect, that he is interested in having others similarly connect with him personally as well.

In his short book, *The Tone of Teaching* (2003) Max van Manen explores some of the other qualities of this personal, non-specialized tone or atmosphere by focusing on one particular, moment or act occurring between self and other, student and teacher: the relational act of shaking hands. This is an act that can be formal, but is at the same time. There is of course no special training or certification for this kind of social interaction, but at the same time. Regardless, a handshake can be seen as indicating a great deal about one's character and personality. Van Manen describes a handshake taking place between a gradeschool teacher and a student, but simultaneously, he implicitly asks his reader to reflect on experiences of other handshakes and acts of greeting:

> … *the classroom door is wide open and the teacher stands in the doorway. She greets him with a warm handshake and a gentle nod. "Good morning, Mark." She notices that he is holding a book … and she is immediately interested. Mark beams with pleasure and anticipation. (2003, p. 30)*

The moment of the handshake, whether it is part of an initial introduction or a daily greeting, can have layers of experiential and sensory significance. It involves touch, in the taking, grasping and "shaking" of another's hand, and sight, in looking the other in the eye. It also involves the body as a whole in a relational act, requiring it to be in close proximity to that of the other. For both persons engaged, these experiential dimensions all meet in the eyes, the grip, and the bodily presence of the other. Awareness, in other words, is focused and gathered at the point where two bodies, two hands, and two sets of eyes meet. And this has the effect, experientially speaking, of establishing and singling out a common time and a "shared space." In describing this dynamic further, van Manen generalizes the handshake to encounters between persons:

> *In each true encounter there is a moment of mutuality that shuts out the rest of the world. In it lies the possibility of genuine interpersonal contact. As our hands or smiling faces respond to the gesture of each other's approach, we create shared space. The smile is experienced as an invitation to openness. Our eyes meet, and for an instant we are there only for each other. (2003, p. 33)*

Space and time are no longer scattered in the myriad "heres" and "nows" that can be presented on the computer screen, and they are also not projected to an imaginary location that may be invoked through a work of fiction. Instead, they are focused and gathered at a single here and now of an interpersonal encounter.

It is this momentary gathering that makes it possible for each of those shaking hands to gain access to the other. Whether it is the "look" of the eyes, the sweat of the palm, or some other corporeal attribute, our bodies express our inner situation in the kinds of relational moment exemplified in the handshake. The access that each person simultaneously allows for the other is in these contexts is particularly open and can be unexpectedly revealing. It is obviously not subject to the craft and careful preparation, for example, that can be invested into writing. "In a handshake," as Carina Henriksson observes, "our lowest of motives may be given away... the deepest secret may show in our eyes; our attempt to hide something may be laid bare in our body language" (2003, p. 14). It follows that a handshake is practiced not only as a first step in getting to know someone else, but that it is also customary to "shake on a deal"—even with an established acquaintance—or to see a truce between enemies as "sealed" through a handshake.

The subtle yet powerful mutuality of the handshake exemplifies a kind of intercorporeal contact that can be said to reappear in more diffuse form in similar relational moments and practices. Moments in which students are addressed and acknowledged as they enter the classroom, or the simple act of going around in a classroom, and asking each student to introduce himself or herself can be laden with similar significance. If only for a few seconds, each student has the undivided attention of the teacher and at least some of his or her classmates. Each student is asked to disclose something about himself or herself, be it through a glance, gesture, or a few words, with the knowledge that this disclosure will be mutual and reciprocal when others in the class have had their turn. In this sense, introducing oneself, or greeting and saying goodbye, is also more than just a familiar ritual or a little "trick" to get students talking in a class or to satisfy some unwritten social contract. Whether the moment of mutuality of verbal address or physical contact is momentary and brief, unexpected and awkward, or deeply affected, it reveals something about the student, the teacher, and, in this sense, also about the class. It may be expressive of an element of reserve and uncertainty, or speak emphatically of enthusiasm and confidence. The introductory ritual equips the teacher with the sense, for example, that he or she should launch into challenging aspects of the curriculum, or to slacken the pace and engage in a review.

### Ambivalent Authentication

Further aspects of encountering the other—online or off—can be explored by expanding the account of computer conferencing initiated above to include first-person responses to what is being posted:

> *Gilles, the teacher, has written an eloquent online introduction that is clearly inviting, but I still can't help ask myself: "How can I possibly come up with my own message like that?" Since the discussion is to continue over the course of the week, I decide to wait for a day or two. The next time I check the online forum, I see the following list of indented names and times:*
>
> *Welcome [Forum: Week 1 Discussion]*
>    1. *Gilles Simon (Sun, Oct. 5, 2008, 07:34)*
>    2. *Maria Plummer (Mon, Oct. 6, 2008, 10:50)*
>    3. *Dan Merceau (Tue, Oct. 7, 2008, 20:14)*
>    4. *Gabriel C. Rifon (Tue, Oct. 7, 2008, 20:18)*
>
> *I click on each of the names and read the corresponding greeting or introduction. As I do so, I find myself double-checking the names of the people, in a deliberate effort to associate the contents of each message with its author. From the introductions, I see that the students who have posted so far are from different parts of the country and, indeed, the world. I also notice that the last two messages were sent in the last couple of minutes. I decide that there's still a little time to wait and find out what else happens before I post my own introduction.*

As each student submits his or her introductory message, the exact time of its submission is recorded, and each message is listed precisely in the order that it is sent. The level at which each message is indented, moreover, indicates the message to which it is ostensibly written in reply. (In the listing above, Maria replied to Gilles's message, and Dan and Gabriel replied to Maria's.) However, despite this detail and precision, the question remains: What exactly is the connection between the names listed and the people they represent? Technically speaking, the answer to this question is fairly straightforward: Each student's name is associated with the person writing and sending the message through user accounts, through a process of "authentication" —providing a password and a "logon" or "user" ID or *identity*. Once a person is authenticated or logged in, that person's name is associated with everything he or she does, whether it is the act of composing and sending a message, or even (as pointed out in chapter one) simply viewing content or postings. As a critical process through which a name is associated with a person or a body, and through which a continuous online identity is established and ensured, this process of authentication deserves further attention.

As is suggested in words like "authentication" and user "identity," the connection between the user ID online and his body, his online persona and his offline "self," is at once important and tenuous. Logging in through a user account is a way of establishing and tracking identity, and of generally connecting the embodied personal identity offline to actions and communications occurring online. For example, if a person's name, password, and similar information are stolen, the perpetrator is able to effectively present himself and undertake decisions and actions as that person. Correspondingly, to act in this way is to commit the crime of "identity theft": the victim's online identity has been effectively taken away from him or her, with all of its potential for action and agency. If one is able to "personalize" the profile information that is associated with one's ID and password, one of the first options that is generally available is to create a kind of "corporeal surrogate" online by posting a selected personal photo, or constructing a visible avatar, and often also by specifying a list of attributes (that are also otherwise generally communicated corporeally) including gender, nationality, and age.

If identity, individuality, and its authenticity are emblematized or embodied online by the "name" that is assigned to a person when he or she logs on (and by whatever attributes that may be associated with that identity), then it is clear that there is a broadly similar way in which presence and identity are "authenticated" offline—namely, through the body: I am recognized as being present in the classroom through my bodily presence just as I can be said to be present in the online class when I have logged on to the Web site or the discussion board or chat space. Correspondingly, Merleau-Ponty describes the body as having a "positing" character: it is, he says, "our anchorage in the world" (2002, pp. 122, 167). Speaking simply and fundamentally, the body posits and anchors an individual's presence in particular time and place. As we shall see, this positing or anchorage works in many different ways, and can serve many different purposes simultaneously.

Just as the handshake and the carefully constructed welcome message involve rather different dynamics in initially establishing a relation between self and other, so too do the user ID and the body. The face-to-face meeting and handshake exemplify the role of the body in anchoring the person individually in the world in a very different way from does a fixed name or a set of attributes specified as a part of an "online identity." Encountering and recognizing someone—whether he or she is a recent acquaintance or an old friend—is much more than a question of matching age, gender, and other corporeal and facial attributes to a person or to that person's name. It is instead a matter, one might say, of "being in their presence," which brings with it a number of implications—both commonplace and far-reaching— that I will now explore.

In *Embodiment and Education*, Marjorie O'Loughlin reiterates an important—but also contentious—affirmation that is an important starting point in this exploration. She says that, "we do not merely *have*" bodies—as one possession among many others—but rather that we "*are* our bodies" (2006, p. 4; original emphasis). O'Loughlin explains this assertion by saying that "an indispensable part of people's identity is manifested in their bodily dispositions, habits, and abilities or skills" (p. 65). These dispositions, habits, and abilities range widely in nature. They extend from what a person does physically and/or socially in a given situation, through what he or she may be wearing, to the attitude to which he or she may be giving clear (or more often, ambiguous) physical expression.

Imagine a student arriving late, avoiding eye-contact from behind a pair of sunglasses, and immediately making his or her way unprepossessingly to the back of the room. Such a student has, of course, "said" something about himself or herself. On the other hand, a student who finds a place at the front of the room and chats nervously with her peers before the class begins communicates a rather different message. The point, of course, is not to identify positive or negative behavioral types and stereotypes. The point instead is that the body, its actions and prepossessions form an intimate, complex, and ambivalent part of the self. These actions and prepossessions, their significance or interpretation is often ambiguous and subject to revision. However, when these same impressions are reinforced through repetition or bodily habit, they can rapidly become much less ambivalent.

Should the two students act in the way mentioned above only once or twice, a teacher might dismiss such behavior as incidental; should they engage in these (or similar) actions three or four times in a row, a teacher would be much more inclined to interpret such behavior as habitual, as expressive of an established trait of character. At the same time, this ambiguous, habitual kind of evidence is rather different from what is provided by the symbols of writing and online messages: Spoken and written words can be insistent and can attempt to persuade or convince. Students coming in early or late can state or insist that they are eager to be in the course. However, the (repeated) presence or absence of their bodies speaks in a very different, ambiguous but powerful way of their enthusiasm and dedication, or lack thereof.

In addition, it goes without saying that a student's body (unlike her ID or "presence" online) can only be in one place at one time. One's attention can certainly drift in class, but any such wandering is strictly limited by the "anchoring" provided by the singular and unsubstitutable here and now of the body in the classroom. The online educational vocabulary of "anyplace" and "anytime" underscores the fact that Internet environments operate differently. As indicated in chapter four, the online world often involves multiple "heres" and "nows"—manifest in multiple windows and widgets—in addition to the habituated, physical "here" and "now" of the computer user at the keyboard and in front of the screen. To be in a classroom, and to actively share it with others, implies that the classroom is also the locus of one's experiential space and time. To be attentively and bodily present somewhere in this sense is to have excluded a myriad of other possibilities, other places and times where one could also "be." Consequently, it is possible to say that one's bodily presence or absence in a classroom speaks of one's commitment in a way that simply logging into a Web site from a screen and keyboard somewhere does not. In coming into the classroom, student and teacher are both physically absent from all other contexts and situations. Online, as is often said, individuals can be "present" but still literally in "anyplace" or at "anytime," with their commitments and priorities also located elsewhere.

It is often said that "actions speak louder than words," and in face-to-face contexts, the body of course is the "means" through which we speak through our actions. To be embodied is to act through the body. Our engagement in the life-world or world of the experiential occurs through the body: "The body," Merleau-Ponty says, "is our general medium for having a world." Attention, awareness, and "consciousness," as Merleau-Ponty emphasizes,

> [are] not a matter of "I think" but of "I can…" [it] is being-towards-the-thing through the intermediary of the body…. Sight and movement are specific ways of entering into relationship with objects [through the body] and if, through all these experiences, some unique function finds expression, it is the momentum of existence [itself.] (2002, pp. 159, 160)

Consciousness, Merleau-Ponty asserts, is not simply awareness per se. It is instead consciousness of what one does and can do; and this doing or performance, moreover, is accomplished through the body. Consciousness, awareness, and attention are in this sense profoundly embodied, rendered unthinkable apart from the body. However, in fulfilling the "function" that Merleau-Ponty says is the "momentum [of our] existence," the body does not just act or perform as a machine would. Our gestures, movements and actions—whether talking, walking, writing, or working—are not just a matter of cold calculation and perfunctory efficiency. Instead, our actions are charged with stylistic and expressive significance. As already indicated, Merleau-Ponty characterizes the body as being "essentially an expressive space" (p. 169). Examples of the two students in class mentioned briefly above illustrate both the complexity and unavoidability of the expression that occurs through the "space" of the body. Sunglasses, eye contact, timing, movement, location, and many other expressive elements combine in a kind of complex layering of conscious and unconscious, cultivated and uncultivated aspects of appearance and expression. These elements are neither purely a matter of awareness nor just a matter of its absence. They include habit, style, character, custom, and disposition and other aspects of personhood that emerge through an inextricable mixture of freedom and constraint presented by our situation. Of course, they also involve aspects of our appearance that are subject to more explicit and directly, conscious control, such as one's hairstyle or clothing. Communication theorist Klaus-Bruhn Jensen (2010) describes the body and its accoutrements as constituting a kind of "productive and receptive medi[um] of communication" on its own (p. 66). He explains:

*First, all human actions can be considered communications in their own right. They may be intentional statements, or incidental behaviors with which others associate meaning, or they may belong to the considerable grey area in between the two ... we continuously communicate with each other through clothing and other visual appearances, body sounds, and general conduct. ... humans are forever ascribing meaning to their cultural as well as natural environments. As ... Paul Watzlawick... put it, humans "cannot not communicate." (p. 66)*

The expressive or performative aspect of the body and its accoutrements, and the infusion of these "performances" with both individual style and significance, has been a matter of special interest among theorists of gender and of the politics of the body. They have recognized that the body, its performance (or conversely, its inability to perform where disability, convention, or other factors may prevent it) plays an important role in constructing and communicating gender and social power. Some argue, contrary to O'Loughlin's claim, that we are not simply our bodies, and that the relationship between identity and the body can be fraught and indirect, both ideologically and practically speaking. Others, such as Judith Butler, emphasize that embodied performance—including the roles, gestures, tones, dispositions, and comportments—is indispensable in the construction and communication of gender. Using the specific term "performativity," Butler makes the case that gender—and by extension other aspects of social identification—is articulated in a focused and intensive way through the body and through the style and expression that are inseparable from it:

*Embodiment clearly manifests a set of strategies or what [can be] called a style of being or... "a stylistics of existence." ... In this sense, gender is... an identity, instituted through a stylized repetition of acts. Further, gender is instituted through the stylization of the body and, hence, must be understood as the mundane way in which bodily gestures, movements, and enactments of various kinds constitute the illusion of an abiding gendered self. (Butler, 2004, pp. 154, 156)*

It is important to note that we are not free to opt out of the "stylistics of existence" that Butler sees as extending from fashion to the stylized repetition of characteristic acts: To engage in a repertoire of gesture and movement that would avoid stylization would itself be expressive of a stylistic choice that can be understood in terms of gender and other facets of identity.

In the case of these embodied aspects of identity and selfhood, the difference between face-to-face and online is very clear: Expressing one's social status and gender through an intricate "stylistics of existence" is very different from indicating them through a specific logon ID and online profile. The expressive power of the body is much more variable, direct, potent, and at the same time, ambiguous, than the more explicit and sometimes pre-set indications about identity and selfhood permitted online.

## An "Ambiguous Mode of Existing"

The body, then, not only allows us to sense things and others in the world, it is also the marker that identifies us and that provides many ways to be either subtly or overtly expressive of who we are. As illustrated in the example of the handshake, discussed above, these aspects are mirrored both in and through the body in terms of its capacities for expression and receptivity, sensing and being sensed—as they intersect in significant moments of relation. Therein lies meaning for education and for the further deepening of significant differences separating online and face-to-face engagement: The body has an expressive directness that evades the artifice of craft and control that is characteristic of writing and other forms of selective self-representation. Whether it is through a handshake or some other means, one's entry into class or one's introduction of oneself to another, the body manifests an inescapable connection to performance and deed. The body does not insist or protest, but through its action, it "speaks louder than words." Moreover, through its performances, the body provides evidence to those around it that is at once ambiguous and powerful.

Merleau-Ponty emphasizes this difficult ambiguity by saying, in effect, that the body is never just one thing; rather, it is always more than the sum of its parts or enumerated functions:

> The problem of…one's own body consists of the [simple] fact that it is all there.… The experience of our own body… reveals to us an ambiguous mode of existing. [Its various] functions'…cannot be interrelated, and related to the external world, by causal connections, they are all obscurely drawn together

*and mutually implied in a unique drama. Therefore the body is not an object. For the same reason, my awareness of it is not a thought, that is to say, I cannot take it to pieces and reform it to make a clear idea. Its unity is always implicit and vague. It is always something other than what it is... (2002, pp. 230, 231)*

It is impossible to overstate, in other words, the complexity and multiplicity of the articulation of identity and selfhood through the body. While no single aspect that is essential to the self or its identity is simply reducible to the body, the body's unavoidably expressive and stylized character simultaneously is always giving expression to these aspects—always already occurring both in its performance and its passivity. At the same time, the fact that these multiple, layered significances of the body are often taken for granted makes them difficult to bring to explicit attention and understanding. Figuring out what the absence of such a manifold and multi-faceted and functional entity that is the body means for online contexts, actions, and interactions is not an easy matter. In taking up this challenge, which is also central to the next chapter, I will focus on the experience of silence, in both online and offline communication. It serves as an example that I believe can help to discriminate between the two from the perspective of pedagogical value and practice.

# CHAPTER 7

# Pedagogy and the Relational Dimension

IN THE PREVIOUS CHAPTER, I LOOKED AT THE ROLE OF THE body in the context of relation with others. Face to face, this role is manifold, subtle, and often implicit, emerging through multiple layers of conscious and unconscious significance and "performance." Online, an equivalent is provided by one's ID and profile, and also by the words of one's messages. These words can provide a powerful resource for manifold and subtle significance, but words also bring with them an emphasis on explicit meaning: skilled writers can manipulate and hone them to evoke a particular atmosphere or to set a certain tone. These kinds of online communications, however, are dependent on preparation and skill in a way that "embodied performances" of style, tone, and even gender, are not. I emphasized that embodied communication involves a spontaneity that is difficult if not impossible to prepare or craft in advance.

This chapter focuses on pedagogy, specifically in terms of the experiential and relational pedagogy mentioned at the end of chapter three. This is the last chapter in the book to present descriptive, experiential evidence directly. It also initiates a more philosophical discussion of the significance of the implications of this experiential evidence—a discussion that continues into the final chapter in this book. The description provided below continues the narrative account of an online course that started in the previous chapter. It also provides a basis for a further and more in-depth discussion of experiential, relational pedagogy implied in the "non-expert" cultivation and setting of tone:

*The next day, I log into the course discussion forum and note that a large number of other students have introduced themselves. I'm also surprised to see that Gilles, the instructor, has started a new thread with a message titled "Let's Begin!"*

*[Forum: Week 1 Discussion] Article No. 1: posted by Gilles Simon on Wed., Oct. 8, 2008, 11:16*
*Subject: Let's Begin!*

Hello All,

Now that most of you have introduced yourselves, I will mention a few things about the class and the first week of readings.

First, let me say how glad I am to already have so many students of such varied backgrounds in this course! I see that we have teachers, like Gabriel, Susan and Joan: together, you obviously bring considerable pedagogical interest and expertise to the class. We also have a number of people with interest and knowledge in technology, including Don, Sasha and Gerhardt. Still others bring experience in online tutoring and administration. And then of course, there is Maria: you are an avid blogger as I am; and we probably both spend "most of life online," as you say.

Given the diverse backgrounds of those who have introduced themselves, let me ask how you would each be inclined to initially define distance education. The UNESCO definition cited in our text (p. 13) defines this type of education as "a system and a process that connects learners to distributed learning resources." But are these systems and processes primarily pedagogical, administrative, technological, or of a different character altogether? Please discuss by replying to this posting (or to others' replies to it).

—Gilles

This message, the second sent by the instructor in the course, exemplifies a number of practices and strategies that are frequently recommended for teachers in online discussion forums. These include being "responsive," replying "swiftly to every contribution … by referring to the author's comment in the conference" (Feenberg, as quoted in Paulsen, 2003, p. 65). Gilles correspondingly greets each of the students who has posted thus far by name, and acknowledges how their individual contexts are relevant to the course. A second technique is evident in Gilles's attempts to "summarize" or at least reference "assigned readings online," and to "make the material relevant" by connecting it to students' professional and personal concerns (Berge, 1995). After discussing the backgrounds and professional experience of the students, Gilles asks how these different backgrounds relate to the systems and processes that their textbook has defined as being constitutive of distance education. Perhaps most importantly, the practice "weaving"—of "responding to several [messages] at once by weaving them together"—seems to be widely recommended (e.g., Mason & Kaye, 1989; Berge & Collins, 1995; Salmon, 2004) and also amply illustrated in Gilles's message: He manages to integrate no less than seven references to student contributions.

Recommendations and techniques for moderating online discussion provide further evidence of the supportive and personal qualities that, as I earlier mentioned, are characteristic of relational, experiential pedagogy. The specifically personal and relational quality of this experiential pedagogy is, of course, illustrated by the practice of referencing students by name and by acknowledging their contributions individually—in an effort to recognize them, in effect, in their personal uniqueness. This recognition, moreover, is one in which each student is acknowledged in a positive or affirmative tone, in terms of the interests and strengths that he or she brings to the class.

The above analysis highlights what can be identified as a further important quality of this relational pedagogy. In addition to the relation between the student and teacher being characterized by a personal emphasis, and a positive tone and atmosphere, a relation of a pedagogical nature also has a tendency to be "non-specialized." For example, the relation between Gilles (above) or Per (chapter one) and their respective student(s) is not principally defined by specialized knowledge or expertise. In Per's "humorous glance" and as expressed by his comfortable patience, for example, Per is not taking up the role of a doctor or a psychologist, and he is not basing his actions and decisions the handicapped student's particular disability or diagnosis. Similarly, for Gilles's recognition of his students to be authentically personal, he needs to see his students first and foremost as persons, rather than exclusively in terms of organizational or human-resource categories that may be implied by the types of jobs they hold (e.g., administrator, technologist, teacher). They are persons who cannot be reduced to any set of technical, administrative labels.

Yet another general quality of experiential and relational pedagogy is the "other-oriented" character of Gilles's latest message. This message is not oriented to Gilles himself, and to his own needs and concerns; instead, the message seeks to be open to or to draw out the situation and concerns of others. Even though Gilles has introduced himself and has described his background in an earlier message, his current message concentrates almost exclusively on the backgrounds of the students. The central question that he poses in this message, moreover, is raised in direct relation to what the students have said about themselves and their backgrounds. The teacher, in other words, is concerned much more with the experiential realm or life-world of the student than he is with the world constituted by his own professional and personal experience.

This final characteristic highlights a deliberate kind of imbalance in the relationship between self and other, student and teacher. Although I have emphasized the importance of reciprocity and mutuality in the description of relational acts like the handshake, the relationships between teacher and student illustrated above is not completely mutual; it is not marked by a fully-balanced reciprocity or equilibrium: One could say that this particular relationship between self (teacher) and other (student) is one in which the teacher is there more for the sake of the other, the student, than the student is there for the teacher. The pedagogical relationship between student and teacher, in other words, is characterized by a certain asymmetry, in which the teacher carries much greater personal responsibility and obligation for the student and for the relationship as a whole than is expected (especially initially) from the student.

### The Sound of Silence—Online and Off

The passage below picks up the online communications between Gilles and his students a couple of weeks later. It presents a discussion that has developed and deepened, and it begins by addressing a message sent by a student named Gabriel:

*Gabriel, I appreciate your honest discussion of your frustration with computer technology. I've been giving it some thought, and know that I certainly can remember (still) struggling with formatting text using online forms, or sometimes hitting "return," as you say, and "wondering where the darn message went." Hmm…*

*More generally, I see how anxieties and unfamiliarity with computers, with writing, and even the computer mouse and keyboard can determine whether people can participate online or not. It is another, more subtle manifestation of the "digital divide" that we read about earlier. Joan, for your part, you describe how your mother eventually gave up on the Web and email because, as you explain, "she just couldn't get comfortable using a computer or even a typewriter at her age." Perhaps you could say that she was subject to a kind of generational divide.*

*Maria and Dan, since you have been silent for a while :-), I invite your response in particular: I was wondering whether you or someone you know have had similar challenges related to a technological divide of some kind— working with differences that separate some people or students from what we assume to be technologically "normal?"*

*—Gilles*

Like the earlier messages from Gilles, the message above can be seen as illustrative of significant, experiential aspects of the pedagogical relation. Perhaps the most evident and also most important of these is its consistent emphasis on engagement with or openness to others: Although the message describes some of the instructor's experiences related to computer anxiety or unfamiliarity, it does this to recognize and confirm Gabriel's "honest discussion" of his/her own frustration with computer technology. It also uses this recollection as an occasion specifically to address two other students who have been silent, and to encourage them to contribute as well.

In the message, the instructor also uses a number of techniques to cultivate what has earlier been identified as a positive "atmosphere" or "tone"— what could also be called a sense of personal or even emotional immediacy or proximity. In accordance with guidelines for online moderation and with online etiquette (netiquette) generally, the message uses a "smiley" or an "emoticon" to indicate levity when requesting a response from two students who have not recently contributed. In this message, as in his earlier messages, Gilles continues to "address students by name"; and going one step further, he "requests [the] responses" of specific students who have fallen silent.

However, it is on the question of silence, the silence of specific students, and silence in pedagogy more generally on which I would now like to dwell. Silence in online discussions poses a significant challenge, problem, or dilemma. An article on "the meanings of silence" for online teaching captures this by providing an experiential account by a teacher identified only as "E":

> There's an extraordinary lack of courtesy. I mean, they don't let me know anything, they don't reply to my e-mails, they don't reply to my messages in the forum! There's just this awful, sort of silence. So, it's incredibly harrowing for the teacher. They don't realise or I'm sure they wouldn't do it. (Benfield, 2000)

Silence, in this teacher's experience, is discourteous, "awful," and "incredibly harrowing." It is an experience she thinks students would not willingly or knowingly impose on her. It is, therefore, not surprising that texts offering guidance to teachers and moderators of online discussion present a range of strategies to either eradicate silence once it has cropped up, or to prevent its emergence altogether. Berge and Collins, for example, advise instructors to "ask less outspoken individuals to participate more actively, and call on specific individuals just as a teacher might call on a student in a traditional class (1995). Feenberg and Xin advise teachers as follows:

> Silence [sends] a message that is both brutal and ambiguous, far more so than the subtle uses of tone of voice, expression and gesture on which we normally rely. The solution to this dilemma is explicit meta-communication. Whenever problems arise, participants must overcome their inhibitions and request further explanation of unclear remarks, call attention to information overload, request clarification of emotional tone and intent, suggest changes in the rules of the forum, and so on. (Feenberg & Xin, 2002)

Silence online is "brutal and ambiguous" as Feenberg and Xin explain, not because it shows that people are overloaded, distracted, or are feeling uninterested or even censured. It is because silence can potentially mean all of these things and more, and all at the same time. It is often impossible to tell whether a student's failure to contribute to the discussion is due to technical difficulties, lack of time, to lack of interest or motivation, illness, or to other circumstances. In addition, it is impossible to tell in some conferencing systems whether a silent student has accessed the forum at all. Listings of messages often do not indicate who has read the messages, or which contributions have been read repeatedly and which have been ignored. Moreover, without posting a message to an online forum, it can be technically challenging to address that person directly: If I do not post a message, then a linked reference to my name will not appear in the conferencing area, and there will be no "reply" options appearing above it that would allow others to "address" me. Consequently, the act of not contributing online is clearly a "dilemma" as Feenberg and Xin describe it or "incredibly harrowing" as the teacher known as "E" puts it. In addition, because someone's silence can be respectful, attentive, embarrassed, hurt, or even passively aggressive, online silence has a problematic ambiguity that can easily render it "brutal"—or at least decidedly negative—in its effect.

This interpretation is instrumental in explaining the significance of "lurking"—the act of reading messages without posting oneself, or of "eavesdrop[ping] on a chat room or conference" (Cybertionary, 2011). In early online usage, and in off-line contexts, this term carried a clearly pejorative meaning. Among other definitions, *Merriam Webster's* describes "lurking" as "lying in wait, especially for an evil purpose" (2010). When I am "lurking" on the Internet—figuratively lying in wait in an online classroom—I do not share the same vulnerability or openness as those from whom I am hiding or for whom I am waiting. I cannot be as easily addressed as those who have already posted, and whose messages and names populate the forum. As a lurker, I am able to read messages online, but I am effectively concealed, and I provide no indication as to the reasons for my concealment. At the same time, everyone in the conference is still led to suppose that I am able to see everything that they are doing and saying. In fact, this type of silent waiting and watching may be carried out by many people at the same time. For example, in the online discussion described above, it may well have been the case that many other students (in addition to the first-person narrator) were earlier waiting and watching—wanting to see what would happen in the online discussion before sending off their first posting. One might say that this "simultaneous" lurking represents a kind of "silence" among multiple people. However, unlike a collective silence in a room, it is a manifestation of silence in which individuals are participating without actually being explicitly aware that their silence is being shared.

The physical presence of the body in the classroom involves sharing that same space with other students and the instructor. Saying something or even remaining silent in a classroom or a similar physical setting involves a kind of vulnerability and trust that is part of this shared bodily presence. Being bodily present in class means that I can be addressed and asked a question—if not by the instructor then at least by my neighbor. This address or question, moreover, can be directed in kindness, indifference, or even hostility. One assumes or trusts that this address will be positive or at least neutral, rather than hostile or threatening. In his discussion of "disembodied telepresence" on the Internet, Hubert Dreyfus makes a similar point:

> You have to be in the same room with someone and know they could physically hurt or publicly humiliate you and observe that they do not do so, in order to feel you can trust them and make yourself vulnerable to them in other ways. There is no doubt that telepresence can provide some sense of trust, but it seems to be a much-attenuated sense. (2008, p. 68)

If it is the case that trust—and the sense of vulnerability that underlies it—is "attenuated" or lessened when one is communicating with others via a video and audio link, then it is perhaps also the case that the degree of this attenuation is altered when text or another mode of communication is used. Experientially speaking, noting the absence of contributions in a small window in the corner of one's screen is rather different from the "dead air" that might find its way into an exchange over the phone or in other audio communication. Newer technologies allowing two or more people to be in audio connection (e.g., conference calling, skype, ELuminate) can drop callers, produce latencies or delays, and block (or fail to block) the background noise that enters in with some participants' connections. These difficulties or situations can be said to increase the ambiguity of silence in these contexts. Silence still has communicative significance, separating words and allowing for turn-taking—or even indicating a thoughtful pause or serving as a kind of "pregnant silence." However, these types of significance always arise in competition with silence—either as a dilemma or a technical problem: Is everyone on the line still there? Is everyone fully engaged in the discussion?

Have they been distracted by events happening around them? Has some-one said something to upset the other person? Or is everyone experienc-ing technical problems of some kind? Similar questions might apply more emphatically in the context of online chat, in which silence of one or more participants takes the form of the cessation of regular textual contributions.

Silence in a physical classroom brings with it a different set of ambigui-ties and also possibilities. Even if a student is silent in a classroom, he or she is still bodily present. The dynamics of this kind of silence of the classroom are illustrated in the descriptive passage below, the last and one of the most important to be considered in this book. It depicts a grade ten class in which the topics of alcohol consumption and alcohol abuse are being addressed and focuses on an unexpected development:

> ... Richard, who usually sits in class with a detached gaze, suddenly became animated. He blurted out that it is hard to talk with your parents when they start relaxing with drinks as soon as they come home from work. "My mother is not really herself after she starts drinking," he said. The effect of his sudden outburst was amazing. Abruptly the whole class went quiet and looked at him. This was so out of character for quiet Richard.
>
> But rather than ridiculing him they seemed to feel how he had risked him-self. Then others, too, shared their experiences with alcohol and how friend-ships get ruined because of what happens when people become inebriated. As the kids were talking, it occurred to me how marvelous it was that they could share their vulnerabilities in this atmosphere of acceptance and togetherness. (Li, 2002, p. 26)

This passage describes an unexpected but deeply personal contribution to a class discussion by Richard, a student who is normally detached and quiet. It has a remarkable effect on everybody in the class: Turning to look at the student, they abruptly fall "quiet." They cease their talking—in other words, they become silent. Richard's sudden and initial contribution and the responses that follow from it have the effect of generating what the teacher characterizes as an "atmosphere of acceptance and togetherness." This posi-tive and affirmative atmosphere is only one of a number of elements in this rich passage that resonate deeply with issues the non-specialized, personal and "other-oriented" relational qualities associated earlier with "relational pedagogy." The emphatically personal character of the event is highlighted at several points where Richard's (perhaps disquieting) personal characteristics of detachment, non-participation are used to explain the response of the teacher and the class. Richard's unique personal characteristics are of clear importance in this explanation. Both the non-specialized and other-oriented qualities in this moment are evident in the way that the teacher responds to Richard's contribution, to the silence that follows, and to the discussion that finally emerges: The response is remarkable because it is not characterized by a particular verbal intervention, but it appears as an act of active and reflective listening: "As the kids were talking, it occurred to me how marvelous it was that they could share their vulnerabilities. . . ." Such a response is non-specialized in that it involves no specific, specialized technique or act of expert categorization; rather, it entails a sense of what is appropriate and what the class is able to handle. It takes the form of a kind of silence that is seemingly indicative of a personal openness and attentiveness. This teacher's response is other-oriented in that it allows students to supportively speak of their hardships, and to "share their vulnerabilities" without being structured or refereed in any explicit way.

The class's initial silence, as well as the teacher's subsequent silence while the class discussion unfolds, illustrates how silence, as a phenomenon, does not need to be either simply passive nor entirely "negative"—experienced, for example, as an undesirable lack. Silence is shown to be not simply the absence of an opportunity, authority, or occasion to speak. It is also not just the opposite or absence of "noise," as a kind of ambience or backdrop that would be a necessary precondition for clear and effective communication, nor does the silence in the classroom entail the harrowing uncertainty or the brutal ambiguity of the absence of textual (or other) information or data, as it does online.

## The Philosophy of Silence

The initial silence of the class and the silence of the teacher that follows can be interpreted in terms of a kind of "philosophy of silence" that has been articulated by phenomenologists and philosophers over the course of the twentieth century. One important contribution to this philosophy is provided by Bernard Dauenhauer's (1980) book-length phenomenological study of silence in which he focuses on "positive" or "significant silences"—silences that are "neither muteness nor mere absence of audible sound" (p. 24). Dauenhauer describes and analyzes four basic but sometimes counterintuitive attributes of such "significant silence": First, this type of silence is connected to speech and is mutually dependent on it; second, it represents an active performance that is not simply the result of habit or reflex; third, silence of this kind does not arise through one or more persons' intention, plans, or premeditations; and fourth, this silence does not represent an act "upon" another, but instead, underscores a connection between self and others that takes the form of a kind of "yielding" to the other (see 1980, p. 24). In this section, I reconstruct Dauenhauer's analyses of these characteristics and also relate them to the students' and the teacher's silence described above.

Moments of "significant silence," according to Dauenhauer, are "active human performance[s]" (p. 24) that arise in intricate interrelationship with speech—"always appear[ing] in connection with an utterance" (p. 24). Silences of this kind can separate a pointed question from a thoughtful answer, or appear as an intimate conversation trails off into stillness. It is significant that both silences manifest in the description of the classroom above occur in intimate interrelationship with the utterances of others. The first, of course, arises from Richard's speech or sudden disclosure, and the second arises while the teacher is marveling at the students' "utterances" concerning their own worries and vulnerabilities.

Second, this kind of silence is also not simply "reducible to reflex behavior" (p. 24); it is more than just an automatic response to a particular stimulus: "However habitual the performance is," Dauenhauer explains, "all performances of silence are in some measure active" (p. 24). In this sense, the two "positive" or "significant" silences described above are obviously not explicable in terms of the mere absence of speech or communication. They are not expressive of passivity in a simple or unmitigated sense, but instead they clearly have a conscious, self-aware, and active dimension to them.

Third, active performances of this kind are not the result of anyone's explicit decision, work, or will to be silent. Such silences "cannot be…performed by an individual acting alone," as Dauenhauer puts it (1973, p. 26):

*Phenomenally... silence [of this kind] shows itself as an act that cannot be performed in radical independence. Someone must indeed act for there to be silence. But he must act in concert with someone or something which is fundamentally distinct from him. (Dauenhauer, 1980, pp. 24–25)*

The silence of the class that follows Richard's disclosure, for example, is of a very different kind that might follow the teacher calling the class to order. No one person, neither student nor teacher, explicitly calls for or requests the silence. Instead, it is a silence in which students act in concert, at the same time, without being told or agreeing in advance to do so.

One of the ways of understanding how silence can be at once unpremeditated and also a concerted act or performance is to consider the relationship of this silence to everyday plans and categories, in other words, to "intentionality." As I will show later, the significance of these kinds of silences lies in part in the dissolution or suspension of intentionality that coincides with them. Their importance arises from the fact that they are not simply reducible to any one meaning, intention, or purpose—any call or plea on the part of one or more persons, or any specifiable intentional impulse.

Fourth, silence in this sense is a spontaneous act involving all of those present; as a result, it can be said to "bind" and "join," those present (Dauenhauer 1980, p. 24). Because a silence like the one following Richard's disclosure is entered into in a manner that is uncoerced and unpremeditated, it has the unplanned effect of underscoring a kind of connection between those who "fall into" it. In this sense, it can be said to "bind" and "join" the students and the teacher together. Comparable to the significance of silence itself, the precise nature or meaning of this connection cannot be given any single, definitive explanation or explication.

Although silences of this kind represent an "active performance," the kind of concerted "act" or "deed" that is performed is decidedly understated. These silences do not take another as their object; they do not act "upon" someone or something. Dauenhauer says that they achieve a sort of unforced "yielding": "silence shows itself as a *yielding* which binds and joins" (1980, p. 24, emphasis added). Falling silent in this way is to give way or to yield. However, precisely what is being yielded to? In the case of the class's silence following Richard's disclosure, what is being yielded to would have to include the significance of Richard's situation, and even the significance of his sudden disclosure of it. In the case of the teacher's attentive silence "as the kids were talking," this silence can be said to represent a receptivity or a "yielding" to the students' willingness to be open and vulnerable. Quoting the description itself, one might say that the teacher's silence is a yielding before the "*atmosphere* of acceptance and togetherness" that emerged after Richard's disclosure. In the case of both silences, the yielding enacted through silence is a giving way to what others are saying or doing. The "doing of silence" in this sense "opens me to the other," as Dauenhauer puts it (p. 24, 1980).

In this context, "the other," Dauenhauer continues, "needs my yielding to reach me" (1973, p. 28). Furthermore, this otherness to which the self yields in silence, Dauenhauer explains, "is beyond one's control" (1980, p. 25). In the silence of the class, prominent elements of otherness or alienness that are beyond the students' and the teacher's control include Richard's situation, as well as his possible role as a victim of his parents' habits. However, it also includes Richard's act of trusting and sharing with others. In the case of the teacher's silence, otherness or alienness is represented in the class's response to what Richard is saying. The teacher's yielding to this otherness or alterity can be seen as a recognition of something that she cannot control and also does not wish to try to control or limit. Insofar as it is a yielding that is necessary for the class to reach her and to reach out to one another, it also has the potential to join or to bring self and others into closer connection.

Moving beyond Dauenhauer's four characteristics of significant silence, it is important to note that the meanings of silences emerge with the power and ambiguity of meanings of the body. What is being communicated, reinterpreted and understood in the description of Richard's disclosure is emphatically embodied: the mutuality of the risk and exposure that is communicated and explored is also the mutuality of embodiment. The site of silence that the students share is in a sense also the shared intercorporeal space they share through their embodiment. One might say that in or through these kinds of "meaningful silences," it is the bodies participating in that silence that are foregrounded and that are given a chance to speak. Van Manen (1991) describes how this meaning can unfold, and how bodies can be expressive in the absence of speech in his description of silence as a way that teachers can work "tactfully" in the classroom. Van Manen explains that the teacher's tactful silence in classroom contexts can have a range of significances (while at the same time avoiding other meanings):

> It may involve a quiet trustful acceptance (while not interrogating or probing the child's mood), or a resolute turning away (while not really leaving), or an unobtrusive lingering presence (while not being demonstrative or purposive about being there for the child). (p. 177)

Of course, a silence that foregrounds one's embodied presence can incorporate more than one of these meanings—just as it is the case that the silence of the class (and of the teacher) in response cannot be reduced to any single, final meaning. Silences of this kind, like the bodies whose physical co-presence they require, tend to be as powerful and ineluctable in their meaning as they are manifold and subtle. In an article specifically on "the sound of silence in pedagogy," Zembylas and Michaelides write that "positive" classroom silences of these kinds are associated the fact that "the majority of students' emotional communications take place without talk" (2004, p. 200). In this sense, they say, such silences "may create meaningful spaces in which emotions (such as anger and hatred) can be reinterpreted" (p. 203). Classroom silences of these kinds, Zembylas and Michaelides continue, "can…indicate a kind of unspoken understanding" or "can be the manifestation of…fear of self-exposure through speaking openly" (p. 203). It seems likely that the class's silence described above incorporates both of these meanings: the students in Richard's class are likely afraid of risking what Richard has risked; but at the same time, the discussions that follow show that a kind of "unspoken understanding" that affirms mutual respect and openness has begun to emerge in that silence.

As already indicated, what is reinterpreted and communicated in the "meaningful spaces" presented by the class's silence is not anger and hatred, but rather, feelings of vulnerability and mutual vulnerability. Students are vulnerable to the destructive shortcomings and habits of their parents and other adults, and they are simultaneously vulnerable to one another. In *The Tact of Teaching*, van Manen describes the kind of space granted through significant classroom silences as ones in which the student or the child is

able to "come to him- or herself." This kind of silence, van Manen continues, "is the silence of patiently waiting, being there, while sustaining an
expectant, open, and trusting atmosphere" (1991, p. 177). This patient and
sustaining "being there," of course, happens through the body, precisely
by its indubitable and persistent but not necessarily insistent or intrusive
presence.

## The Silent Demand

The phenomenon of silence features prominently in a text of the Danish
philosopher Knud Løgstrup (1997) who speaks of a kind of silent "call"
or "demand" that arises when the self is addressed by another person face-
to-face. In being addressed by another, as Løgstrup describes it, a person is
placed in a position to respond—in a position, in other words, of *responsibility*. In this way, Løgstrup develops an account of the ethics of interpersonal
relation—an ethics which can help contextualize the classroom silences
described in the previous chapter, and ultimately, to tie together many of
the experiential, relational attributes described as above as distinctive for
pedagogical practice.

Løgstrup focuses first on questions of address and response, and on the
way in which a type of ethically-charged challenge or "demand" for response
emerges from these questions. He explains that any question or address,
however meek or kindly it may be communicated, presents an implicit
request or demand to the person to whom it is addressed. Løgstrup describes
this "ethical demand" by referring to it first as a kind of "unarticulated" or
"silent demand." It is a "demand implicit in every encounter between persons," Løgstrup explains, but it is also "not vocal" (p. 22):

> *Regardless of how varied the communication between persons may be, it always*
> *involves the risk of one person approaching the other in hope of a response...*
> *in every encounter ...there is an unarticulated demand, irrespective of the...*
> *nature of the encounter. (p. 18)*

Løgstrup is careful to indicate that the silent demand implicit in every communication is not an unspoken expectation to simply respond in some way
to the address or to answer to its explicit content. "This demand," Løgstrup
emphasizes, "is not merely for a response to what we say...it is not to be

equated with a person's expressed wish or request" (pp. 15, 21). Instead, what is implicitly or "silently demanded" in the other's address is a recognition of the other; what is hoped for is a responsible entry into a relation with the person who has made the address. This demand is articulated not in terms of the content of the address itself, but in the dispositional or attitudinal terms of a particular atmosphere, tone, or "note" that Løgstrup says is also implicit in an address:

> In conversation...we deliver ourselves over into the hand of another. This is evident in the fact that in the very act of addressing a person we make a certain demand of him. This demand is not merely for a response to what we say.... What happens is that simply in addressing him, irrespective of the importance of the content of what we say, a certain note is struck...by our very attitude toward him. [And in this way we]... step out of ourselves in order to exist in...relationship with him. For this reason the point of the demand—though unarticulated—is that as the note struck by the speaker's address is accepted, the speaker himself is accepted. For a person inadvertently or even intentionally not to hear the note in what we say, therefore, means that it is we ourselves who are being ignored.... (pp. 15, 21; emphases added)

Løgstrup explains here that when the other addresses me, he or she is silently demanding something of me through the attitudinal or dispositional tone or note of his or her address. Through this tone, the person who has made the address puts himself or herself in a position of risk or trust. This dynamic is all the more significant because the demand made by the other, as Løgstrup indicates, is not simply a demand or request to receive a response. It is a silent demand to be recognized and addressed as such, to be validated as a person or as another.

Dauenhauer expresses similar thoughts in discussing "utterances" and the "appeal" that any one utterance necessarily makes beyond what is said in order to achieve what he calls its "authentication":

> At bottom, in all utterance there is an appeal beyond the utterance for an authentication of the utterance. No utterance is ultimately and definitely authenticated by another utterance or set of utterances... Authentication must be awaited in silence. Whatever is uttered is either validated or

*invalidated [in this way.]* (1980, pp. 19–20)

Like Løgstrup, Dauenhauer is saying that any address is an appeal for recognition and authentication, and that such an appeal goes beyond language into silence. Tied to every question, every address, is the appeal to be recognized and authenticated. Furthermore, this appeal could not simply be said aloud, by stating: "I am appealing to you to answer the question I just asked." Such an explicit demand simply begs the question, asking again tacitly and silently for another response, recognition, or "authentication."

In the shared relational space opened up by an embodied silence, for both Løgstrup and Levinas, an "address" "appeal or "demand" arises that somehow "binds" self and other. Løgstrup, as well as other phenomenological ethicists such as Emanuel Levinas (e.g., 1998) and Bernhard Waldenfels (e.g., 2007) all understand this call, pretense, claim, or demand as the foundation for human ethical engagement. They see ethical, relational responsibility as arising from these elemental moments in the encounter between self and other, when one, in effect, addresses another as "you." During this encounter, moreover, silence and, by extension, the silent and vulnerable presence of the body are indispensable.

### The Call of the Other: One Response

As abstract as this description of the encounter of self and other through silence may appear, its weight is easy to demonstrate in concrete terms. These kinds of terms are provided in the story of Richard's disclosure and of the class's (and teacher's) response to it. As a first example, Løgstrup and Dauenhauer say that what is important in the call or demand of the other is not so much its explicit content as that which is expressed in "the note struck by the speaker's address"—an expression that must be waited upon "in silence." In the description of Richard's disclosure, the importance of his simply saying something and the note that he strikes in saying it is clearly evident. Richard's disclosure is described as coming from someone who usually sits "in class with a detached gaze." The tone of his contribution is described as an animated "outburst" occurring very "suddenly" and being "blurted out." A distinctive note is obviously struck through this appeal that, as Dauenhauer says, subsequently awaits recognition or "authentication …in silence" (1980, p. 20).

For this silence to be a "positive" or "significant" in the senses described by Dauenhauer, its validation—as well as the possibility of its invalidation—need to be genuinely at stake. (Indeed, the stakes could not be higher, since as Løgstrup says, if "the note in what we say" is ignored, it "means that it is *we ourselves* who are being ignored.") These stakes are communicated powerfully as the teacher notes in her description: "Abruptly the whole class went quiet and looked at him. This was so out of character for quiet Richard. But rather than ridiculing him they seemed to feel how he had risked himself." Judging from the teacher's own words ("But rather than ridiculing him…"), a less than positive response from the class seems to be a distinct possibility—and it is not difficult to imagine the silence in the description being broken by stifled guffaws or derisive whispering.

Instead, the silence in the classroom seems to manifest a particular kind of hesitancy, indecision, and uncertainty. It appears that the validation of Richard's remark and of Richard himself is indeed at stake. Like the co-present bodies upon which it depends, this embodied silence can be said to bring with it aspects of disposition or comportment, of tone or atmosphere: Like the body as an "expressive space," this silence is ambiguous and ambivalent in what it expresses, but also like the body it cannot not be expressive. In its indecision and uncertainty, this particular silence can be said to be expressive of a disposition characterized, in part, by openness and receptivity.

As indicated earlier, because its meaning is not actual or determinate but rather ambiguous and diffuse, this moment of silence can be said to represent a kind of disruption of what has been labelled as "intentionality." The silence expresses and enacts a disruption of the connection established between the self and the world by the self's plans, priorities, meanings, and categories. These plans and categories can be seen as momentarily suspended or dissolved in the hesitant, surprised silence of the class. It appears that the students in the class are not sure how to understand, classify, and how to incorporate Richard's comment and also their own responses into their intentions, interpretations, and actions—regardless of how short-term and tentative these intentions may be. Indeed, it is through such a suspension or dissolution of order, categorizations and purpose that it is possible to encounter the other, or what can also be referred to as the "alien." Waldenfels explains:

> By itself… [intentionality] does not leave sufficient room for the alien as the alien. Intentionality means that something is intended or understood as something, that it is taken in a certain sense. Anything that might be alien would [thus be] conceived in such a way that it is reduced to some part of a sense-whole…. (2007, p. 22; original emphasis)

The alien would not be truly alien or "other" if it already neatly fit with or could be fully assimilated to the goals and ends of the self that encounters it. I illustrated this dynamic, using rather different terms and examples, in my discussion of the in-school and online dissection. However, the description of the class's silent encounter with Richards "alien-ness" goes noticeably further. Unlike the reactions to the dissection, the response to Richard's disclosure is not simply to label or categorize it with labels like "gross," "weird," or "strange." Instead, these and other terms and responses are suspended altogether. If the events in Richard's classroom could be made part of a "sense-whole" or of something that "made sense," it would lose its "alien-ness" and effectively be reduced to the terms of the self. The class would simply carry on as it had before. However, the alienness that is represented in Richard's remark, to use Waldenfels's terms, can be said to resist "any attempt to insert it into a local grid which would be accessible to everyone." Instead, as Waldenfels continues, "it can only be reached by crossing a certain threshold" (2007, p. 8). One could say that the surprised silence of the class—and the watchful silence of the teacher that follows—represent a kind of suspension of categories and intentions that is entailed in approaching just this threshold.

## A Pedagogical "Praxis of Silence"

This way of understanding the relationship between the self and the other, between the familiar and the alien—or between what I am doing and another's demand for pause and recognition—is foundational to the way that pedagogy is articulated in this book. Speaking specifically of the encounter between the teacher and the young student or child, phenomenologist Jan Martinus Langeveld emphasizes the centrality of the relationship between the self and the other in education, and its connection to the intentional activities of integrating and assimilating that which is encountered in the other:

> *The encounter with the other always means the encounter with the unknown. The unknown can be easily misperceived. As a result, the child can be systematically misunderstood, assimilated to the model of that which is known or familiar, and the unknown will consequently be reduced in terms of the grown-up or the cliché. (Langeveld, as quoted in Lippitz, 2007, p. 76)*

It is through pedagogical projects, plans, and activities that the teacher, the self, acts to assimilate the child or the other to "that which is known or familiar." The teacher, understandably, is necessarily compelled to make some "sense" or retrieve some "sense-whole" from a student's or a child's "strangeness." At the same time, though, there are methods for the teacher to avoid this situation—at least momentarily—and can hold these assimilations and reductions at bay. He or she can enact a kind of receptivity and openness that is registered—among other ways—through silence. It is in this sense that the teacher's silence that begins with Richard's disclosure—and that continues "while the class is talking" —can be understood. In this context, the teacher is acting in a way that is pedagogically responsible and responsive precisely insofar as she is not acting, insofar as her response is one of reticence, passivity, and (perhaps most importantly) receptivity.

It is significant that the teacher's response can be most readily defined in negative terms, largely in terms of what is not done, and what does not happen. While silence, as we have seen, is not simply a matter of passivity, it is also easiest to describe silence specifically in terms of what it is not. It is therefore not surprising that educational theorist John Dewey speaks of the capacity for this kind of action specifically in terms of a negative capability. Dewey describes this capability in terms of a trust in "intuitions," and an openness to that which might "come upon" the individual in his or her "immediate sensuous and emotional experiences" (1980, pp. 33–34). Dewey also emphasizes "that this trust should hold even against objections that reflection presents..." (p. 34). What is important in this negative capability, in other words, is a receptivity to what "comes upon" one, rather than active engagement in reflection, critique or other mental activity that would reduce it to an object of thought.[1] What is central to this notion of passive or receptive ability is the realization that inaction can be as important as—or even more important than—explicit acts, statements, cognitions, and communications. It is not what you do by virtue of reason and action that always counts; instead, what you don't do, by virtue of intuition, disposition, and comportment that can be paramount.

Of course, there is no obvious way to "instrumentalize" this type of response, to have a technology or technique to direct and control aspects of this negative capability. For example, although many have written about the meanings of silence in interpersonal relation, no one claims "expertise" in the exercise of silence. There is no specialization in education or pedagogy in the theory and practice of silence. Like the other aspects of relational pedagogy, silence remains a personal and "non-specialized" practice. It is neither a question of presenting an explicit program for action nor of the simple cessation or censoring of one's activity and speech. This negative capability can be said to be exercised in the ambiguous terrain between action and passivity, the place where the "threshold" Waldenfels describes as being crossed in reaching the other can be tentatively located and carefully negotiated. This place can be approached, reached, and sometimes inhabited through a meaningful reticence, in a sustaining unobtrusiveness, or in an engaged openness or receptivity. Zembylas and Micheladies were among the first to describe the approach associated with this ambiguous place in terms of a pedagogical "praxis of silence." In fact, it is the implications of such a praxis—for pedagogical places both online and offline—that I attempt to further explore in the next and final chapter of this book.

---

1    Dewey also explains that he derived this notion of "negative capability" from a letter written by the poet John Keats, who similarly describes this capability in terms of what it is not, namely, as a refusal to act by "reaching after fact and reason," and a capacity simply for "being" in the midst of ambiguities, "uncertainties" and "doubts" (as quoted by Dewey, p. 33).

*section four*

**SPACE OF THE SCREEN AND PLACE OF THE CLASSROOM**

# CHAPTER 8

# *To Each Pedagogy Its Place*

IN THIS CONCLUDING CHAPTER, I CONNECT THE PEDAGOGI-cal, relational, non-specialized, and "negative" praxis of silence with the central question of this book: Namely, "What are the differences separating screen and classroom as spaces (or places) for pedagogy?" I explore the significance of the praxis of silence and negative capability for pedagogy, online and offline, by focusing on five specific points. These five points connect this praxis and capability together with the various attributes of online and offline experience identified throughout the book. By linking these different experiential attributes with some of the key elements of experiential, relational pedagogy—and also bringing them into connection with the questions of space and place—this chapter synthesizes a number of the most important points developed throughout this book:

1. I consider what Løgstrup and Levinas say about phenomena of presence and immediacy, and how their conceptions relate to situations where one is not bodily or immediately present on the Web.

2. I examine the way in which Web technologies impose forms of classification and specialization (as discussed in chapter three) that do not readily accommodate the "non-specialized," even "non-intentional" character of pedagogical practice (described in chapters seven and eight).

3. I focus on the kind of explicit activity and deliberate communication required by Web technologies (as discussed in chapter three),

looking specifically at incompatibility of this communication with the suspension of action, intentionality, and the "negative capability" that are important in pedagogical practice.

4. I outline how Web interfaces that accommodate activity and labor in the form of convenient efficiency and routine procedure (discussed in chapter five), can downplay types of exertion that are pedagogically valuable.

5. Use of technology is consistent with the use of a particular vocabulary, voice, and perspective (discussed in the preface and chapter two) that directs awareness away from the non-intentional, non-purposive, receptive, personal, and ethical attributes of pedagogical practice (discussed in chapter eight).

I consider each of these points in its own separate sub-section within this chapter. I conclude with a discussion of the language of learning and education, describing ways of talking and thinking sensitive to pedagogy conceived of not only as a practice of silence, but also as a practice of ignorance and unknowing.

## The Order of the Sign and the Body

If, as Løgstrup says (and as Levinas and others variously restate), the other is encountered in silence through receptivity to a kind of call, what kind of a site do online technologies provide for such receptivity and silence? Silence, as discussed in the previous chapter, is manifold in its significance face to face, providing a place for the powerfully ambiguous expressive possibilities of the body; but online, it is generally described as a problem to be solved, as terms like "lurking," "harrowing," or "brutal ambiguity" make clear. Do Løgstrup, Levinas, and others exploring the phenomenology of relation see the dynamics of the call and response, self, and other as possible outside of the face-to-face encounters?

Both Løgstrup and Levinas answer this question indirectly, yet their answers are also strikingly similar. Each draws a distinction between the immediate presence of the other and the other's mediation through a "representation" or "picture." Løgstrup, for example, warns how, in another's absence, tension or uncertainty can lead one "to form a picture of his character." Løgstrup implies that this picture is then used to explain the other's actions and motivations; it is subsequently reinforced and augmented through this process. At the same time, Løgstrup makes it clear that this dynamic can be forcefully interrupted when we find ourselves in the "personal presence" of other:

> However, when we are in direct association with him this picture usually breaks down; his personal presence erases it. It is not erased because of any particular words, deeds, or conduct.... His presence and my picture of him are irreconcilable.... To associate with or encounter personally another person always means to be "in the power of" his words and conduct. (1997, pp. 13–14)

Løgstrup is suggesting that the immediate presence of another has a kind of power or priority over any fixed image or picture formed during his or her absence. Using terms that seem particularly resonant at a time of cyberbullying and flamewars, Løgstrup warns, in effect, that different forms of mediation can create a negative picture that only the other's physical presence, the immediacy of his "words and conduct," can nullify, shatter, or erase.

Levinas, for his part, understands the "image" or "representation" as coming into being not so much through physical absence or distance, but rather, he discusses these matters in the slightly more abstract terms of cognitive or conceptual distance. He sees the very acts of assimilation, categorization, or even "cognition" (all characteristic, in their own way, of intentionality) as posing a challenge in terms of response and responsibility of the self vis-à-vis the other. As Levinas puts it, it affects the "urgency" manifest "between me and the neighbor" (1981, p. 87):

> The neighbor's presence summons me with an urgency so extreme that we must not seek its measure in the way this presence is presented to me, that is, manifests itself and becomes a representation. For this still, or already, belongs to the order of images and cognition, which the assignation overwhelms. Here urgency is not a simple lack of time, but an anachronism: in representation presence is already past. (1987, p. 120; emphasis added,)

The presence of the neighbor, of the other, is so extreme in its immediacy and urgency that it is betrayed by any intentional, reflective, conceptual activity that might follow from it. The other's presence is so direct or immediate, as Levinas says, that it actually "overwhelms... the order of images[, of] cognition" and of the sign. The "representational" processes of knowing and thinking must always play catch up in the face of this presence. It is something, he adds, that "intentional analysis does not" and cannot "account for" (1987, p. 118).

Just as with Løgstrup, Levinas implies that communication explicitly relying on representation and mediation—such as reading, writing, and other processed and transmitted forms—are qualitatively different from immediate presence and contact. Levinas comes close to making such a claim outright, when he speaks of "contact" (i.e., communication involving a kind of physical presence) with the neighbor as the "ethical event of communication:"

> *The contact in which I approach the neighbor is not a manifestation or a knowledge, but the ethical event of communication which is presupposed by every transmission of messages, which establishes the universality in which words and propositions will be stated.* (1987, p. 125)

Transmitted or mediated messages—signs, representations, words, or propositions—rely on the primary "ethical event" of direct "contact" between self and neighbor. The transmission of any specific message, Levinas is saying, is only possible because of the contact implied in a prior and even primal "ethical event of communication" that transmission presupposes. Significantly, Levinas refers to this encounter with the neighbor by using the phrase "face to face," or by referring to it simply as "the face." Levinas defines "the face" and the "face to face" as being precisely that which is "immediate"—as the "way in which the other presents himself, exceeding *the idea of the other in me*" (p. 50, original italics). The body and the sign, in other words, could be understood as constituting two different orders or broad sets of possibilities and limitations for experience and relation: To the body belongs receptive presence that is open to a direct and immediate contact with the other, while disruption, deferral, and distortion of immediate presence belong to the realm of the sign.

Taking Levinas's and Løgstrup's words literally would seem to allow little opportunity for pedagogy online—particularly as it has been described in the experiential, relational terms in this book. Pedagogy is about a non-specialized, ethical, and asymmetrical relationship between a self and an other, e.g., a teacher who employs negative capability to cultivate a supportive atmosphere, ultimately only for the sake of the others in the class. The Internet, on the other hand, is reliant on mediation, representation, and signification, processes anathema—according to Levinas and Løgstrup—to the ethical event of contact and silence through which the demand of the other is articulated.

However, Levinas's use of the terms "face" and "face-to-face" should not be understood in strictly literal terms, nor should Løgstrup's opposition of presence and picture be understood as an absolute opposition. It is not as if the ethical significance of the "call" of the other simply ceases to exist online altogether. Even though it is not possible to "call" or "call on" someone in an online discussion (as it is to do on the street, on the phone, or even with live chat), responsive and responsible encounters between the self and the other do clearly happen in these forums. Although they have different experiential qualities, online encounters are not somehow devoid of authenticity, risk, or the potential for care. I believe that some phenomenological critiques of online education, such as that of Hubert Dreyfus, have floundered precisely by making these kinds of broad and direct claims about what separates online and offline education. However, as I have shown in previous chapters, particularly chapter seven, the fundamental characteristics of relational, experiential pedagogy can be readily identified as being present in online discussions: teacher and students can work to set a positive tone or atmosphere for the class; the teacher can orient himself or herself to students in a way that is in keeping with the asymmetrical, other-oriented character of pedagogy; and these types of practices can be enacted in a manner that is (to a degree, at least) both personal and non-specialized.

Levinas's and Løgstrup's distinctions, then, do not provide a definitive or final answer to the central question of this book. The differences separating screen and classroom, experientially and pedagogically speaking, are not are simple as saying that one is "of the sign" and that the other is "of the face." That would be to falsify the experiences, for example, of atmosphere, of non-specialized and other-oriented relations that clearly can occur online. Keeping the figurative rather than the literal import of Levinas's and

Løgstrup's distinctions in mind, the question can be answered by looking elsewhere. It is my contention that the figurative significance of Levinas's notion of "the face" and Løgstrup's understanding of the silent demand emerges fairly clearly and cogently by reviewing some of the other experiential, relational pedagogical qualities noted earlier in this book.

### Specialization and Unspecialized Receptivity

In considering the second point listed above, the question of the specialization implied in the use of Web (and other) technologies, and the non-specialized nature of pedagogical activity, it is important to recall how Web technologies foreground their own "function": In contexts of online education, different configurations of Web technologies are referred to explicitly as specific tools suited to quite different educational and communicative ends. For example, one tool will be for chatting, a second specifically for collaborative document development, and a third for more specialized "knowledge building" activities. In a physical setting, of course, these different ways of communicating and collaborating could be carried out simply by using a room with table and chairs—thus with little or no emphasis on or reference to tools and their specialized functions. Moreover, what is particularly important experientially and pedagogically in such settings, both online and offline, is what can be accomplished with a relatively generalized and non-specialized skill set. As illustrated in some detail in chapter seven, among the tasks that are accomplished through these non-specialized or personal skills and abilities is the cultivation of a "tone," "climate," or "atmosphere" that is positive and supportive and that is conducive to participation and engagement.

Also, as discussed in chapter seven (and additionally in chapter eight), the type of subtle and intricate but personal and non-expert work involved setting a tone or cultivating an atmosphere differs online and offline. In offline contexts, the work involved in "tone setting" is generally a matter of the many elements or layers of an ambiguous but strongly expressive embodied "presence" (elements such as gesture, disposition, and tone of voice). Online, skills such as those as required for typing, composition, and verbal description take their place. Unlike the more spontaneous abilities involved in embodied presence, these writing and compositional abilities rely on the premeditated application of "craft," skill, and learned abilities:

a message can be crafted and carefully revised before it is posted, and the skills and abilities used in this crafting and revision are generally acquired (at least in part) through formal education and training. Thus, the first important distinction drawn in this study between spaces and places for pedagogy online versus offline is an emphasis on explicitly categorized specialization of functions and abilities versus a tacit non-specialization that can cover a potentially wide range of functions and purposes. In this distinction, the offline classroom clearly appears as a place that is suitable for pedagogical practice. Online contexts, by contrast, impose forms of specialization and classification that need to be consistently combated and counteracted by both students and teachers.

## Negative Capability

I identified another distinction that further separates online and offline by focusing on the body's ambiguous but strongly expressive character that appears with special clarity specifically in relationship to silence. Online communicative places or spaces emphasize the active exercise of learned skills, and correspondingly, they also de-emphasize or render difficult more passive or receptive types of engagement that are not explicitly taught or communicated. I explored this distinction through an in-depth examination of the possible roles of silence in pedagogical contexts, both online and offline. In spaces and places that are offline and embodied, silence can serve many purposes, both positive and negative; but significantly, these purposes include ways in which availability, receptivity, and openness are communicated. Especially as a collective or shared experience, silence can serve as a place of yielding to that which is other or alien—whether this "other" takes the form another person, or of previously unexplored embodied feelings, whether these be feelings of vulnerability or visceral emotions associated with "squeamishness." Online, silence tends to have a rather different range of significances, with many of these being clearly negative, as expressed in the terms "lurking" or "lurkers," used to describe those who are silent in online discussions, or in descriptions of these silences as being "brutal" or "harrowing" in nature.

What is rendered very difficult if not impossible by the connotations of silence on the screen is the realization of what I referred to in the previous chapter as a person's "negative capability." This refers to the capacity to be receptive, open, and available. It also refers to capacities that are foregrounded not in overt action and communication, but in contexts where inaction, reserve or reticence are important. By requiring users to log on, to click here versus there, to choose some words but not others in composing and submitting explicit communications, Web technologies repeatedly foreground explicit action over inaction. In this sense, online technologies simply cannot match the unavoidable force, nuance, and multiplicity of the body as an "expressive space." Text, of course, is complex and manifold, but it too often requires one to insist, for example, "I'm here for you," while one's actual, indivisible, indubitable embodied presence requires no such insistence.

Considered together with the first point (about the implicit exercise of non-specialized skills offline), this second distinction makes it possible to draw some conclusions about the different places and spaces made available in the classroom and on the screen. If place is germane to rest and stasis, to the absence of overt activity, then the physical classroom is in this sense akin to place. It is a place in which silence can express receptivity, and in which reticent withholding can be a valuable pedagogical act, in and of itself. By contrast, the computer screen and online environments generally are much more readily comparable to space, as inviting, perhaps even insisting on, explicit action and interaction: Online experience unfolds in locations in which silences associated with stasis and rest is rendered problematic, and in which it is not possible or easy to distinguish between passive presence and the simple probability of absence.

### Spaces and Places for Pedagogy

A distinction between online spaces and offline places is further reinforced through the fourth point outlined above, the idea that the space of the screen is geared toward convenient efficiency, whereas the classroom has no such evident bias. This point was illustrated by the comparison of the experience of simulated and laboratory dissection provided in chapter five, which showed the rather different nature of physical entities encountered online and offline: The virtual dissection is grounded in design goals defined in service of the user's priorities or intentionality; the in-school dissection, in contrast, involves an encounter with ends utterly alien to these plans

and purposes. This examination further underscores the parallels identified above between Tuan's and Casey's analyses of space and place, and the
respective sites of screen and classroom. Space, like the environment of the
computer screen, is associated with efficiency, action, and motion. Having
"neither history nor a future" (Shields, 2003, p. 51), the virtual space of the
screen is uninhibited by the precedents of others' use and actions, and unen-
cumbered by the often nonnegotiable claims of the past (or even the future).
This virtual space is endlessly "refreshable," effectively devoid of friction,
and thus specially suited to effortless action and motion that is suggested by
terms like "browsing" or "surfing." It tends to have, on practical and technical
levels, the characteristics of "blank environments" or "neutral tabula rasa"
that Casey associates with space as abstract mathematical or geometric extension. By way of contrast, the offline world, with its many encumbrances, its
variegated but binding history and its singular but unresolved future, again
falls on the side of Tuan's and Casey's descriptions of place.

Considered pedagogically, not simply convenience or efficiency, motion
or activity, in and of themselves are important. Instead, it is the pedagogical value of that which is encountered that is of paramount importance—
whether it is encountered in a context of encumbrance and confinement
or in sites designed for convenience and "brilliance." In the one, students
accustomed to computer technology encounter a quite familiar and pliable
context that is already integrated into their understandings of who they are
and of their place in the world around them. In the other, students may
encounter what is unfamiliar, obtrusive, and alien to their everyday purposes and plans as intentional beings.

In the chapters that followed this initial discussion of the encounter
with "otherness," I showed how the dynamic between the self and the other
is foundational to experiential pedagogy. Whether the "alien" or "other"
is encountered in the surprising organization of a creature's viscera, or in
the silent appeal or demand articulated through another's call, the task of
pedagogy is defined in terms of appropriate receptivity and response to this
other and its claim upon the self. This relationship between the self and the
other is foundational the pedagogical relation between student and teacher,
a relation that is in many ways *sui generis*. It is different, in other words,
from (nearly) all other relations: It is oriented to the other in a way that

relationships generally are not. It is not simply defined in terms of professional responsibilities, but it also has a non-specialized and personal dimension. It relies on practices and capabilities that are not acquired through specialization or enacted as a set of "positive," enumerable competencies. Understood in this way, pedagogy, in its experiential, relational dimension can certainly take place on the space of the computer screen—with its frictionless efficiency and insistence on explicit activity—but is much more suited to the place of the classroom, with the possibilities that it offers for receptive inaction.

## Languages of Technology and Pedagogy

In this concluding section, I deal with the fifth, last, and in many ways most important of the points listed at the beginning of this chapter: the perspective, voice, or vocabulary encouraged through technology and technological talking and thinking that directs awareness away from the non-intentional, non-purposive, receptive, personal, and ethical attributes of pedagogical practice. In dealing with this issue, I hope to develop, from my discussion of silence passivity and receptivity, a number of conclusions about education more generally. In the preface, I talked about how the issues raised by offline and online for pedagogy lead to central questions about pedagogy and technology more generally: It is these central, general questions that I now will raise and tentatively address.

Throughout this book I have shown in various ways that education is experientially about the relation between self and other. This other can be a quasi-other that may be the subject matter for study, but it generally takes the form of a human "other," another person, student, or teacher. This person, by definition of their role, is to be oriented to the student as other, giving her or him the freedom and opportunity to manifest her otherness. This characteristic of being oriented to the other, of non-purposive openness and receptivity, is not only more difficult to enact in technologically mediated contexts, but is made more difficult to recognize, reflect on, and discuss in the context of experience and language that is ever more influenced by technology and technological thinking.

In the preface, I explained that the vocabulary of "signals," of perceptual and communicative "data" and their effective "recording" and "transmission" provide a kind of language for understanding, discussing and addressing communication in a wide range of settings. Whether this vocabulary arises in the context of empiricist conceptions of experience or contemporary discourses of learning as cognition and knowledge construction, the result is much the same. Communication and cognitive phenomena are understood as the transmission, collection, and analysis of data. In chapter two, I indicated that this vocabulary is representative of only one of many different perspectives for knowing and acting. Education becomes a question of the conditions for the optimal encoding, transmission, decoding, processing, and (re)construction of data or information. Specifically, it is illustrative of independent objective knowledge of the third person perspective (singular or plural)—rather than, say, the collective life-world knowledge and activity of the first-person plural, or the ethical implications of the second-person singular. In chapter three, I considered the further ramifications of language in exploring how it at once reflects the enframing nature of technology by itself, foregrounding the technical, functional character of the phenomena in question. For example, these technologies force their users to choose between different communicative modalities or functions—such as chat, discussion, voice, video—where no such choices are imposed by our own bodies and voices. This is also the case, of course, for educational and other "functions," such as using computer technology, learning online (or offline), and facilitating processes of use or learning. I also showed that this emphasis on functionalist specialization runs counter to the non-specialized, relational nature of pedagogy. Although there are myriad technical areas of specialization and sub-specialization, there still is no expert with the specialty how to relate to another as a person, and there is no diploma available in cultivating a positive atmosphere with friends or in a classroom.

In foregrounding their functions, sometimes rather insistently, technologies compel us to particular practices while discouraging others. For example, as "solutions" specifically designed to send, receive, and process information, Internet communications technologies find their "*raison d'etre* [in] the efficient transmission of unambiguous information from one individual to another" (O'Sullivan & Flanagin, 2003, p. 77). In this context, it is not surprising that silence has negative connotations: given the communicative purpose of these technologies, it appears as inefficient, sub-optimal,

or counterproductive to not speak or "fill" them with communicative information—if not direct communication, then explicit meta-communication
about what has already been communicated. Speaking in purely technical
terms, silence is obviously manifest in these contexts quite emphatically as
the absence of communication or information. It only follows that to achieve
transmission of maximal technical efficiency, the signs, codes, and representations that are transmitted via these technologies must be kept as free as
possible from extraneous, accidental or meaningless signs, codes, and data
as possible. The accidental or ambiguous information that can interfere with
such transmission is known in technical vocabularies as "noise." The diagram
below, widely known as the "Shannon-Weaver Model of Communication,"
indicates the relationship of noise to the processes of transmission and recep-
tion. "Messages" are transported from sender to receiver in the form of "signals," which are to be kept as free as possible from any sources of "noise."

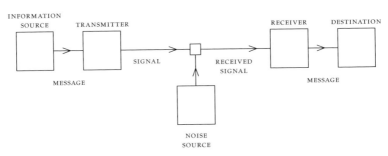

FIGURE 1: *The Shannon-Weaver Model of Communication*

What is most important in the understanding of communication, so eco-
nomically schematized in this diagram, is the inputs and outputs and the
flow between them. Since the optimal transmission of information is the
technology's *raison d'etre*, emphasis is placed on a maximal relation between
what goes into the system (as an input or information source), and what
comes out (at the destination). Optimization or maximization would involve
ensuring that these inputs and outputs always match as closely as possible,
that nothing is lost or distorted as it travels between information source
and destination. Powerfully expressing an understanding of communication
in this way—in terms utility, efficiency, function, and its maximization—a
model like that of Shannon-Weaver leaves little room for consideration of

other aspects of communication, such as receptivity, openness, or negative capability—and of their communicative expression in silence.

In the way that this model—and the accompanying vocabulary of signals, noise, and transmission—frames the question of communication, the phenomenon of silence is effectively rendered moot or useless. Such a diagram presents communication as a question of the effective transmission of signals, and the greatest possible suppression of noise. Speaking not about the Shannon weaver diagram, but of silence in the modern world generally, Max Picard (1952) has observed that

> Silence is [a] phenomenon today that is "useless." It does not fit into the world
> of profit and utility; it simply is. It seems to have no other purpose; it cannot
> be exploited. It interferes with the regular flow of the purposeful [and] ...
> stands outside the world of profit and utility; it cannot be exploited for profit;
> you cannot get anything out of it. It is "unproductive." Therefore it is regarded
> as valueless. (pp. 2–3; emphasis added)

Silence, like the yielding, openness, and negative capability that can be associated with it, has no clear practical or economic utility or value. Picard indicates that, as a result, we have lost track of silence—and by extension, also of the kind of non-intentional, other-oriented dispositions associated with it. A technologically saturated life-world unavoidably reinforces language, conceptions, and ways of acting that are themselves technological. In this context, it appears confusing or counterintuitive to insist on the value of silence as the absence information, or to affirm elements of practice, pedagogy and relation that might be expressive of such silence.

However, the Shannon-Weaver diagram is more than just any model; as one source explains, it can be considered to be the "mother of all models": It presents "a ubiquitous graphical form" that exemplifies the "input-output model," one that shows the flow between a beginning state and a goal or end state. The same source continues: "We are by now so used to the input-output model that we may no longer be aware of its peculiarities... and its weaknesses" (Hollnagel & Woods, 2005, p. 11). This diagram and the way that it represents communication is significant because it is illustrative of general ways of thinking about teaching, pedagogical practice and education. Appearing as the true offspring of the Shannon-Weaver communication diagram, similar models of education, of learning or cognitive processes, and of instructional development abound in the literature of education, and perhaps especially distance education and educational technology.

These diagrams and models are easy to find in instructional design and educational technology texts, featuring, for example, sets of boxes and arrows arranged to represent the "student academic learning model" (Molenda & Pershing, 2008), the "model of online learning" (Anderson & Elloumi, 2004), or the "model of e-learning environments" (Necat, 2007). Like the Shannon-Weaver diagram, these generally map out a kind of operational flow between discrete functional entities, tracing a relationship between inputs and outputs, and in doing so, tacitly calling for its optimization. Such diagrams typically show the passage of a product (e.g., "learning") through a number of stages, trace the flow of data, information, knowledge from one point to another, or outline the contributions of a number of factors to an overall goal or outcome. Moreover, each stage, element, or entity is depicted as a particular, specialized contribution to this goal or purpose. The categorization and compartmentalization in these diagrams also does not recognize the ambiguous and non-specialized functions and contributions that have been shown earlier to be a part of the body and indispensable to relations—pedagogically contextualized or otherwise. Like the Shannon-Weaver model, moreover, what is registered in such diagrams is explicit movement, action, and function—and their contributions to a final, predetermined outcome, product or goal. What is expressed, in distilled, economical form, is the "in-order-to," the relentless functionalist emphasis that Heidegger sees as essential to technology, and that we have seen as highlighted in technical designs, designations, and discussions. In the case of academic learning, educational technology, and other systems diagrams, the aim of the "in order to" is the accrual or attainment of knowledge, the accomplishment of explicit curriculum outcomes, the active demonstration of specifiable and specialized competencies.

In the case of the Shannon-Weaver model, the opposite of explicit information and communication is purely random noise or silence. In the case of an educational input-output model, the diametric opposite of the processes of movement, action, and function outputs (through which student learning and knowledge are achieved) achievement would be stasis, and ultimately, ignorance, un-knowing, uncertainty and inactivity. Ignorance or "not-knowing" is particularly apposite to silence. In the context of educational model—like the Shannon-Weaver "mother of all models"—inactivity and ignorance would, by definition, be seen as anathema to the system. Like silence that is expressive of non-use of the system, these elements would not readily be seen as having any value because they have no readily understandable function. They can only be seen as standing outside of the world of profit and utility and interfere with the regular flow of the purposeful. In the context of "solutions" specifically designed for the purpose of operationalizing inputs through specialized processes, inactivity, uncertainty, and ignorance appear as inefficient, sub-optimal, or counterproductive—as concepts to be eradicated through further careful design and planning. Just as there is no value for communicative silence in the Shannon-Weaver model, or in antecedent systems of educational inputs and outputs, it follows that there is also little or no possibility for the unknowable, inexplicit, inexpressible, or ineffable.

In their study of "the sound of silence in pedagogy" (see chapter eight) Zembylas and Michaelides advocate a pedagogical praxis not only of silence, but also of unknowing and passivity—and in this sense also of the suspension of intentionality that is manifest in openness and receptivity:

> The most valuable contribution teachers and students might be able to make is keeping open the possibility for questioning silences in the classroom and, even more important, for responding in silence. This suggests a pedagogy that is no longer informed simply by knowledge, but by ignorance, unknowability, and the inexpressible. There is definitely a risk involved in this effort, both for students and teachers, because it is sometimes difficult to interpret silences in public spaces; yet it may be a worthwhile risk to take. (2004, p. 210; original emphasis)

Zembylas and Michaelides call for a way of thinking and engaging in education—a pedagogy, in short—that recognizes the value of unknowing as much as it affirms silence. Furthermore, I would argue, elements of such a pedagogy can be found in the attributes of pedagogical relationality described in the previous chapter—including an emphasis on the other, on asymmetry, tone, and "unspecialization." Zembylas and Michaelides's paper and my discussion above recognize and affirm the value of the receptivity, negative capability, and the subtleties of disposition and atmosphere.

Such a pedagogy or praxis, of course, is not purely passive, but based on an understanding that information, learning, speech, is intimately intertwined with unknowing, the unknowable, ignorance, and silence:

> *Thus, a philosophy of unknowing in education reminds us that education remains a game of knowing and unknowing, of learning and ignorance, and, above all, of wondering. Our argument is that in view of a philosophy of unknowing, the whole nature of education has to be rethought beyond "knowledge of facts and theories," with an awareness that educational theory has to take into account a pedagogy that allows for the silence that facilitates openness, receptivity, and hearing of the experience of otherness.* (2004, p. 210)

Facts and theories remain indispensable, however. Therefore, the abstract, functional, and optimized spaces of the computer screen also have their place in education. The very interchangeability, renewability, and convenience of these spaces give them an educational value that is in many ways easy to recognize and affirm. However, they should not be foregrounded at the expense of places and experiences of the embodied, particular, and non-interchangeable. It is to these places and these experiences that we are repeatedly and unavoidably forced to return, by our own bodies and through our relations with others—even as technological experience and terminology become ever more pervasive. These embodied places and experiences, by virtue of their elusive ambiguity, too often escape notice and attention. This subtlety and ambiguity can also be mistaken for something mysterious or even mystical. In the face of diminishing language and sensitivity for places of embodied presence—and the openness and receptivity they allow—it is important to focus on mute and unobtrusive aspects of embodied presence, to develop and also recover ways of describing and understanding these aspects, and to be able to reconnect with them more closely in practice.

# References

Anderson, T., & Elloumi, F. (Eds.) (2004). *Theory and practice of online learning*. Athabasca, Canada: Athabasca University.

Anderson, T., Rourke, L., Garrison, D. R., & Archer, W. (2001). Assessing teaching presence in a computer conferencing environment. *Journal of Asynchronous Learning Networks*, 5(2). Retrieved from http://sloancon sortium.org/sites/default/files/v5n2_anderson_1.pdf

Araya, A. A. (1997). Experiencing the world through interactive learning environments. *Techné: Journal of the Society for Philosophy and Technology*, 3(2). Retrieved from http://scholar.lib.vt.edu/ejournals/SPT/v3n2 /ARAYA.html

Barlow, J. P. (1996). A Declaration of the independence of cyberspace. Retrieved from http://homes.eff.org/~barlow/Declaration-Final.html

Barnacle, R. (2009). Gut instinct: The body and learning. *Educational Philosophy and Theory*, 41(1), 22–33.

Barr, G., & Herzog, H. A. (2000). Fetal pig: The high school dissection experience. *Society & Animals*, 8(1), 53–69.

Barry, John. (1991). *Technobabble*. Cambridge, MA: MIT Press.

Benfield, G. (2000). Teaching on the Web—Exploring the meanings of silence. *STAR Report. Original ultiBASE Publication*. Retrieved from http://ultibase.rmit.edu.au/Articles/online/benfield1.pdf

Benner, P. E. (1994). *Interpretive phenomenology: Embodiment, caring, and ethics in health and illness*. Thousand Oaks, CA: Sage.

Berge, Z. L., & Collins, M. P. (Eds.). (1995). *Computer-mediated communication and the on-line classroom in Distance Education.* Cresskill, NJ: Hampton Press.

Biesta, G. (2006). *Beyond learning: Democratic education for a human future.* Boulder, CO: Paradigm Publishers.

Bleeker, H., & Mulderij, K. (1992). The experience of motor disability. *Phenomenology + Pedagogy, 10,* 1–18.

Bollnow, O. F. (1982). On silence-findings of philosophico-pedagogical anthropology. *Universitas, 24*(1), 41–47.

Bollnow, O. F. (1989). The pedagogical atmosphere. *Phenomenology + Pedagogy, 7,* 5–63. Retrieved from http://www.phenomenologyonline. com/articles/template.cfm?ID=348

Borgmann, A. (1992). *Crossing the postmodern divide.* Chicago, IL: University of Chicago Press.

Brontë, C. (1847). *Jane Eyre.* London, UK: Smith, Elder & Co.

Bruckman, A., & Bandlow, A. (2003). HCI for kids. In J. Jacko & A. Sears (Eds.), *The human-computer interaction handbook: Fundamentals, evolving technologies, and emerging applications* (pp. 428–440). Mahwah, NJ: Lawrence Erlbaum Associates.

Buber, M. (1958). *I and Thou.* New York, NY: Scribner's.

Bull, G. (2009). Tutor, tool, tutee: A vision revisited. *Contemporary Issues in Technology and Teacher Education, 9*(2), 89–94.

Burgess, T.F. (2001). A general introduction to the design of questionnaires for survey research. Retrieved from http://www.leeds.ac.uk/iss/docu mentation/top/top2.pdf

Butler, J. (2004). Performative acts and gender constitution: An essay in phenomenology and feminist theory. In H. Bial (Ed.), *The performance studies reader.* London, UK: Routledge.

Buytendijk, F. J. J. (1988). The first smile of the child. *Phenomenology + Pedagogy, 6*(1), 15–24.

Calvino, I. (1982). *If on a winter's night a traveler.* New York, NY: Harcourt Brace Janovich.

Casey, E. S. (2009). *Getting back into place: Toward a renewed understanding of the place-world* (2nd ed.). Bloomington, IN: Indiana University Press.

Chandra, S. S., & Sharma, R. K. (2004). *Sociology of education.* New Dehli: Atlantic Publishers.

Chiu, K.-Y., Stewart, B., & Ehlert, M. (2003). Relationships among student demographic characteristics, student academic achievement, student satisfaction, and online business—Course quality factors. NAWeb. Retrieved from http://www.unb.ca/naweb/proceed ings/2003/PaperChiu.html

Csikszentmihalyi, M. (1990). *Flow: The psychology of optimal experience.* New York, NY: Harper & Row.

Cybertionary. (2011). Retrieved from http://www.cybertionary.com.

Dauenhauer, B. P. (1973). On silence. *Research in Phenomenology, 3*(1), 9–27.

Dauenhauer, B. P. (1980). *Silence: The phenomenon and its ontological significance.* Bloomington, IN: Indiana University Press.

DBU (Dallas Baptist University). (2007). Retrieved from http://www.online teachingtips.org/

Dede, C., Whitehouse, P., & Brown-L'Bahy, T. (2002). Designing and studying learning experiences that use multiple interactive media to bridge distance and time. In C. Vrasid & G. Glass (Eds.), *Current perspectives on applied information technologies. Vol. 1: Distance education* (pp. 1–30). Greenwich, CT: Information Age Press.

Deka, T., & McMurry, P. (2006). Student success in face-to-face and distance teleclass environments: A matter of contact? *The international Review of Research in Open Learning and Distance Learning, 7*(1). Retrieved from http://www.irrodl.org/index.php/irrodl/article/view/251/468

Dewey, J. (1934/1980). *Art as experience.* New York, NY: Perigee Books.

Dilthey's, W. (1971). *Schriften zur Pädagogik.* Paderborn: Schöningh.

Dobson, T. M. (2002). Keeping in touch by electronic mail. In Max van Manen (Ed.), *Writing in the dark: Phenomenological studies in interpretive inquiry* (pp. 98–115). London, ON: Althouse Press.

Downes, S. (2005, October). E-learning 2.0. *eLearn magazine: Education and technology in perspective.* Retrieved from http://www.elearnmag.org/sub page.cfm?section=articles&article=29-1

Downes, S. (2002) Education and embodiment. Retrieved from http://www.downes.ca/cgi-bin/page.cgi?post=92

Dreyfus, H. (2001). *On the Internet.* New York, NY: Routledge.

Dreyfus, H. (2008). *On the Internet* (Second edition). New York, NY: Routledge.

Dutton, J., Durron, M., & Perry, J. (2002). How do online students differ from lecture students? *Journal for Asynchronous Learning Networks*, 6(1), 1-20.

Feenberg, A., & Xin, C. (2002). *A teacher's guide to moderating online discussion forums: From theory to practice*. Retrieved from http://www.text weaver.org/modmanual4.htm

Feenberg, A. (1989). A user's guide to the pragmatics of computer mediated communication. *Semiotica*, 75(3/4), 257–278.

Feenberg, A. (2004). Modernity Theory and Technology Studies: Reflections on Bridging the Gap. In T. J. Misa, P. Brey & A. Feenberg (Eds.), *Modernity and Technology* . Cambridge MA: MIT Press. Pp. 73-104.

Friesen, N., & Hopkins, J. (2008). Wikiversity; or education meets the free culture movement: An ethnographic investigation. *First Monday*, 13(10). Retrieved from http://www.uic.edu/htbin/cgiwrap/bin/ojs /index.php/fm/

Friesen, N. & Sævi, T. (2010). Reviving forgotten connections in North American teacher education: Klaus Mollenhauer and the pedagogical relation. *Journal of Curriculum Studies*, 142(1), 123-147.

Froguts.com. (2003). Froguts. Retrieved from http://froguts.com/

Froguts.com. (2009). Froguts. Retrieved from http://froguts.com/flash _content/index.html

Gadamer, H. G. (2004). *Truth and method* (2nd rev. ed.). New York, NY: Continuum.

Gagné, R. M. (1962). *Psychological principles in system development*. New York, NY: Holt Rinehart and Winston.

Garrison, D. R., Anderson, T., & Archer, W. (2000). Critical inquiry in a text-based environment: Computer conferencing in higher education. *The Internet and Higher Education*, 2(2–3), 87–105.

Ginsburg, S. (2011). *Designing the iPhone user experience: A user-centered approach to sketching and prototyping iPhone apps*. Boston, MA: Pearson.

Giorgi, A. (2009). *The descriptive phenomenological method in psychology: A modified Husserlian approach*. Pittsburgh, PA: Duquesne University Press.

Harasim, L. (Ed.). (1993). *Global networks: Computers and international communication*. Cambridge, MA: MIT Press.

Hassler, F. (2000). *Student choice for dissection alternatives, experience notebook.* Retrieved from http://www.dissectionchoice.org/notebook.html

Haury, D. L. (1996). *Alternatives to animal dissection in school science classes* (Report No. EDO-SE-96-08). Columbus, OH: Clearinghouse for Science Mathematics and Environmental Education (ERIC Document Reproduction Service No. ED402155). Retrieved from http://www.eric.ed.gov/ERICWebPortal/contentdelivery/servlet/ERICServlet?accno=ED402155

Heckman, R., & Annabi, H. (2003). A content analytic comparison of FTF and ALN case-study discussion. *Proceedings of 36th Hawaii International Conference on Systems Science.* CD-Rom. Washington, DC: IEEE Computer Society Press.

Heidegger, M. (1962). *Being and time.* New York, NY: Harper.

Heidegger, M. (1971). The nature of language. In *On the way to language* (pp. 57–108). New York, NY: Harper & Row.

Heidegger, M. (1977). *Sein und Zeit.* Frankfurt am Main: Klostermann.

Heidegger, M. (1992a). The end of philosophy and the task of thinking. In D. F. Krell (Ed.), *Basic writings, revised and expanded edition* (pp. 431–449). New York, NY: HarperCollins.

Heidegger, M. (1992b). The question concerning technology. In D. F. Krell (Ed.), *Basic writings, revised and expanded edition* (pp. 311–341). New York, NY: HarperCollins.

Hein, S. F., & Austin, W. J. (2001). Empirical and hermeneutic approaches to phenomenological research in psychology: A comparison. *Psychological Methods, 6,* 3–17.

Henriksson, C. (2003). The difference the body makes: The teacher's presence online and offline. *The Journal of Teaching and Learning, 2*(2), 13–22.

Hiltz, S. R., & Shea, P. (2005). The student in the online classroom. In S. R. Hiltz & R. Goldman (Eds.) *Learning together online: Research on asynchronous learning networks* (pp. 145–168). Mahwah, NJ: Lawrence Erlbaum Publishers.

Hollnagel, D. D., & Woods, E. (2005). *Joint cognitive systems: Foundations of cognitive systems engineering.* Boca Raton, FL: CRC Press.

Hooper, P. K. (2008). Looking bk and moving fd: Toward a sociocultural lens on learning with programmable media. In T. McPherson. (Ed.),

*Digital youth, innovation, and the unexpected.* The John D. and Catherine T. MacArthur Foundation Series on Digital Media and Learning (pp.123–142). Cambridge, M A: The M I T Press..

Husserl, E. (1970). *Crisis of European sciences and transcendental phenomenology.* Evanston, I L: Northwestern University Press.

Husserl, E. (1983). *Ideas pertaining to a pure phenomenology and to a phenomenological philosophy: First book: General introduction to a pure phenomenology.* New York, N Y: Springer.

Irrgang, B. (2007). *Gehirn und leiblicher geist. Phänomenologisch-hermeneutische Philosophie* des Geistes. Stuttgart: Franz Steiner Verlag.

Irwin, S. (2005). Technological other/quasi other: Reflection on lived experience. *Human Studies, 28*(4). 453–467.

Jacob, P. (2003). Intentionality. In E. N. Zalta (Ed.), *The Stanford encyclopedia of philosophy.* Retrieved from http://plato.stanford.edu/entries/intentionality/

Jacobs, J. W., & Dempsey, J. V. (1993). Simulation and gaming: Fidelity, feedback, and motivation (pp. 197–227). In J. V. Dempsey & G. C. Sales (Eds.), *Interactive instruction and feedback.* Englewood Hills, N J: Educational Technology Publications..

Jay, M. (2006). The lifeworld and lived experience. In Dreyfus, H.L. & Wrathall, M.A. (Eds.) *A Companion to Phenomenology and Existentialism.* Malden, M A: Blackwell.

Jensen, K.-B. (2010). *Media convergence: The three degrees of network, mass and interpersonal communication.* London, U K: Routledge.

Johnson, D. (1997, May 29). *Frogs' best friends: Students who won't dissect them.* Retrieved from http://query.nytimes.com/gst/fullpage.html?res=9D00E5DF123AF93AA15756C0A961958260

Jonassen, D. H. (2006). *Modeling with technology: Mindtools for conceptual change.* Columbus, O H: Merrill/Prentice Hall.

Jonassen, D. H., Peck, K. L., & Wilson, B. G. (1999). *Learning with technology: A constructivist perspective.* Upper Saddle River, N J: Merrill.

Jonassen, D.H., & Reeves, T.C. (1996). Learning with technology: Using computers as cognitive tools. In D.H. Jonassen (Ed.), *Handbook of research on educational communications and technology* (pp. 693–719).New York, N Y: Macmillan.

Jordan School District. (2004). *4th quarter biology project pig dissection.* Retrieved from http://edublog.sedck12.org/media/blogs/UTIPS /BioPT_C.doc

Joyce, J. (1997). *A portrait of the artist as a young man.* New York, N Y : Bantam.

Jurczyk, J., Kushner-Benson, S. N., & Savery, J. (2004). Measuring student percep-tions in web-based courses: A standards-based approach. *Online Journal of Distance Learning Administration, 7*(4). Retrieved from http:// www.westga.edu/~distance/ojdla/winter74/jurczyk74.htm

Keengwe, J., Onchwari, G., & Wachira, P. (2008). The use of computer tools to support meaningful learning. *Association for the Advancement of Computing in Education Journal, 16*(1), 77–92.

Kolko, B. E., Nakamura, L., & Rodman, G. B. (2000). *Race in cyberspace: An Introduction. In B. E. Kolko, L. Nakamura, & G. B. Rodman (Eds.), Race in cyberspace* (pp. 1-13). New York, N Y : Routledge.

Kozma, R. B. (1987). The implications of cognitive psychology for com-puter-based learning tools. *Educational Technology, 27*(11), 20–25.

Lajoi, S. P. (Ed.). (2000). *Computers as cognitive tools. Vol. 2: No more walls.* Mahwah, N J : Lawrence Erlbaum.

Lakoff, G., & Johnson, M. (1980). *Metaphors we live by.* Chicago, I L : The University of Chicago Press.

Land, R. (2005). Embodiment and risk in cyberspace education. In R. Land & S. Bayne (Eds.), *Education in cyberspace* (pp.149–164). London, U K : Routledge.

Land, R., & Bayne, S. (2005). Screen or monitor? Issues of surveillance and disciplinary power in online learning environments. In R. Land, & S. Bayne (Eds.), *Education in cyberspace* (pp. 165–179). London, U K : Routledge.

Langeveld, M. J. (1983). The "secret place" in the life of the child. *Pheno-menology + Pedagogy, 1*(2), 181–189.

Leder, D. (1990). *The absent body.* Chicago, I L: University of Chicago Press.

Leemkuil, H. H., Jong, T. de, Hoog, R. de, & Christoph, N. (2003). K M Quest: A collaborative internet-based simulation game. *Simulation & Gaming, 34,* 89–111.

Levering, B., & van Manen, M. (2002). Phenomenological anthropology in the Netherlands and Flanders. In A.-T. Tymieniecka (Ed.), *Phenomenology world wide: Foundations—Expanding dynamics—Life-engagements: A guide for research and study* (pp. 278-286). Dordrecht: Kluwer Academic Publishing.

Levinas, E. (1987). *Collected philosophical papers.* Dordrecht & Boston: Martinus Nijhoff.

Levinas, E. (1998). *Otherwise than being: Or beyond essence.* Pittsburgh, PA: Duquesne University Press.

Levine, I. S. (2010). Friendship: The importance of showing up. *Psychology Today.* Retrieved from http://www.psychologytoday.com/blog /the-friendship-doctor/201003/friendship-the-importance-showing

Levy, P. (1997). *Collective intelligence: Mankind's emerging world in cyberspace.* Cambridge, MA: Perseus Books.

Li, S. (2002). Classroom conversation. In M. van Manen (Ed.), *Writing in the dark: Phenomenological studies in interpretive inquiry.* London, ON: Althouse Press. Retrieved from http://www.phenomenologyonline .com/sean/papers/Class_conversation.pdf

Lippitz, W. (2007). Foreignness and otherness in pedagogical contexts. *Phenomenology & Practice,* 1(1), 76–96.

Locke, J. (1690). *An essay concerning human understanding.* Retrieved from http://www.gutenberg.org/cache/epub/10615/pg10615.html

Løgstrup, K. E. (1997). *The ethical demand.* Notre Dame, IN: University of Notre Dame Press.

Lu, Y., Huang, W., Ma, H., & Luce, T. (2007). Interaction and social presence in technology-mediated learning: A partial least squares model. In *Proceedings of Wireless Communication, Networking, Mobile Computing, WiCOM Management Track: Information System & Management, China* (pp. 4411–4414). New York, NY: IEEE.

Lupton, D. (2000). The embodied computer user. In D. Bell & B. Kennedy (Eds.), *The cyber cultures reader* (pp. 477-488). New York, NY: Routledge.

Lye, J. (1996). *Some principles of phenomenological hermeneutics.* Retrieved from http://www.brocku.ca/english/courses/4F70/ph.html

Manovich, L. (2001). *The language of new media.* Cambridge, MA: MIT Press.

Mason, R., & Kaye, A. (1989). *Mindweave: Communication, computers and distance education.* Oxford, UK: Pergamon Press.

McIntyre, R., & Woodruff Smith, D. (1989). Theory of intentionality. In J.

N. Mohanty & W. R. McKenna (Eds.), *Husserl's phenomenology: A text-book* (pp. 147–179). Washington, DC: Center for Advanced Research in Phenomenology and University Press of America.

McPherson, T. (2006). Tara's phenomenology of web surfing. In W. Hui Kyong Chun & T. Keenan (Eds.), *New media, old media: A history and theory reader* (p. 201). New York, NY: Routledge Taylor & Francis.

Merleau-Ponty, M. (1968). *The visible and invisible: Followed by working notes.* Evanston, IL: Northwestern University Press.

Merleau-Ponty, M. (2002). *Phenomenology of perception.* London, UK: Routledge.

*Merriam Webster Online.* (2010). Retrieved from http://www.merriam-web ster.com/

Merrill, P. F., Hammons, K., Vincent, B. R., Reynolds, P. L., Christensen, L., & Tolman, M. N. (Eds.). (1996). *Computers in education.* Boston, MA; Allyn and Bacon.

Molenda, M., & Pershing, J. A. (2008). Improving performance. In A. Januszewski, & M. Molenda (Eds.), Educational Technology: A Definition with Commentary (pp. 49-80). New York: Lawrence Erlbaum.

Mondragon, J. (Ed.) JSD *amphibian curriculum: Frog anatomy.* Retrieved from http://www.sf.adfg.state.ak.us/Static/Region1/amphib/PDFs/student .pdf

Moss, D. (2003). *Hating in the first person plural: psychoanalytic essays on racism, homophobia, misogyny, and terror.* New York, NY: Other Press.

Moustakas, C. (1994). Phenomenological research methods. Thousand Oaks, CA: Sage.

Necat, B. (2007). Distance learning for mobile internet users. *Turkish Online Journal of Distance Education,* 8(2). Retrieved from http://tojde.anadolu .edu.tr/tojde26/pdf/article_3.pdf

Nichols, D. M. (1994). Issues in designing learning by teaching systems. In *Proceedings of the East-West International Conference on Computer Technologies in education (EW-ED'94)* (pp. 176–181). Crimea, Ukraine.

Nivi, B. (2009). How to write an elevator pitch. *Harvard Business Review Blog.* Retrieved from http://blogs.hbr.org/nivi/2009/04/how-to-write -an-elevator-pitch.html

Nohl, H. (1949). *Die padagogische Bewegung in Deutschland und ihre Theorie* Frankfurt a/M: G. Schulte-Bulmke.

Nuutinen, J., Sutinen, E., Botha, A., & Kommers, P. (2009). From mind tools to social mind tools: collaborative writing with woven stories. *British Journal of Educational Technology.* D O I : 10.1111/j.1467-8535.2009 .00973.x

OED [Oxford English Dictionary]. (2007). Oxford, UK: Oxford University Press. Retrieved from http://www.oed.com/

O'Loughlin, M. (2006 ). *Embodiment and education: Exploring creatural existence.* Dordrecht, Netherlands: Springer.

O'Sullivan, P., & Flanagin, A. (2003). Reconceptualizing 'flaming' and other problematic messages. *New Media and Society,* 5(1), 69–94.

Picciano, A.G. (2002). Beyond student perceptions: Issues of interaction, presence, and performance in an online course. *Journal* of Asynchronous Learning Networks, 6(1), 21–40. Accessed May 15, 2008 from: http://www.sloan-c.org/publications/jaln/v6n1/pdf/v6n1_picciano.pdf

Papert, S. (1980). *Mindstorms: Children, computers and powerful ideas.* New York, N Y : Basic Books, Inc.

Papert, S. (1989). Computer as material: Messing about with time. *Teachers College Record,* 89(3).

Paulsen, M. F. (2003). *Online Education and Learning Management Systems.* Bekkestua: NKI Forlaget. Accessed from: http://home.nki.no/morten /index.php/norsk-meny/artikler/mine-powerpoint/doc_download /8-online-education-and-learning-management-systems.html

Pea, R. D. (1985). Beyond amplification: Using computers to reorganize human mental functioning. *Educational Psychologist,* 20, 167–182.

Peppers, C. (2006). The Dangerous Pronoun: An Ecopoetics of "We." *International Journal of the Arts in Society,* 1(2), 93–100.

Picard, M. (1952). *On silence.* Chicago, I L : Regnery.

Picciano, A. G. (2002). Beyond student perceptions: Issues of interaction, presence, and performance in an online course. *Journal* of Asynchronous Learning Networks, 6(1), 21–40. Retrieved from: http://www.sloan -c.org/publications/jaln/v6n1/pdf/v6n1_picciano.pdf

Prensky, M. (2001). "Digital natives, digital immigrants." *On the Horizon* 9 (5) 1-6.

*Random House Dictionary.* (2010). New York, NY: Random House.

Rheingold, H. (2000). *The virtual community: Homesteading on the electronic frontier.* Cambridge MA: MIT Press.

Risser, J. (2010, August). *Where do we find words for what we cannot say? On language and experience in the understanding of life.* Paper presented at the meeting of the International Human Sciences Research Conference, Seattle, WA.

Rosenberger, R. (2009). The sudden experience of the computer. *AI & Society, 24*(2), 173–180. doi: 10.1007/s00146-009-0190-9

Royce, L. (2008). Game review: Dead space. *Bag of Mad Bastards (Blog).* Retrieved from http://bombmatt.wordpress.com/2008/11/06 /dead-space/

Russell, T. L. (1999). *The "no significant difference" Phenomenon: 248 Research Reports, Summaries and Papers* (4th ed). Raleigh, NC: North Carolina State University.

Russell, T. L. (2008). *The "no significant difference" phenomenon.* Retrieved from http://www.nosignificantdifference.org/

Sackville Highschool. (2008). *Specific curriculum outcomes: Oceans [Grade] 11.* Retrieved from http://www.sackville.ednet.ns.ca/Curri culumDocuments/SCOFilesScience/OCE11SCO.pdf

Saevi, T. (2005). *Seeing disability pedagogically: The lived experience of disability in the pedagogical encounter* (Doctoral dissertation). Bergen, NO: Bergen University Press.

Salmon, G. (2004). *E-moderating: The key to teaching and learning online* (2nd ed.). London, UK: Routledge Falmer.

Scardamalia, M., & Bereiter, C. (2003). Knowledge building environments: Extending the limits of the possible in education and knowledge work. In A. DiStefano, K. E. Rudestam, & R. Silverman (Eds.), *Encyclopedia of distributed learning.* Thousand Oaks, CA: Sage.

Scheper-Hughes, N. (1992). Demography without Numbers. In D.I. Kertzer & T.E. Fricke (Eds.), *Anthropological Demography: Toward a new Synthesis.* Chicago: University of Chicago Press.

Scholl, C. (2007). General template rat dissection years 11–12. Retrieved from http://education.qld.gov.au/curriculum/area/science/docs/temp -rat11-12.doc

Sennett, R. (2000). *The Corrosion of Character: The personal Consequences of Work in the new Capitalism.* New York: W. W. Norton & Company.

Shannon, C. E. (1948). A mathematical theory of communication. *The Bell System Technical Journal,* 27(3), 379-421. Retrieved from http://plan9 .bell-labs.com/cm/ms/what/shannonday/shannon1948.pdf

Shields, R. (2003). *The virtual.* London, U K : Routledge.

Slater, D. (2002). Social relationships and identity on-line and off-line. In L. Lievrouw & S. Livingstone. In *Handbook of new media: Social shaping and consequences of ICTs.* (pp. 533–543). New York, N Y : Sage.

Smith, P. L., & Ragan, T. J. (1993). *Instructional design.* Upper Saddle River, N J : Prentice Hall.

Smith, R. J., & Palm, L. J. (2007). Comparing learning outcomes between traditional and distance introduction to philosophy courses. *Discourse: Learning and Teaching in Philosophy and Religious Studies,* 6(2), 205–226.

Solot, D., & Arluke, A. (1997). Learning the scientist's role: Animal dissection in middle school. *Journal of Contemporary Ethnography,* 26, 28–54.

Spiecker, B. (1984). The pedagogical relationship. *Oxford Review of Education* 10(2), 203–209.

Stahl, G., & Hesse, F. (2006). ijCSC—A Journal for Research in CSCL. *International Journal of Computer-Supported Collaborative Learning,* 1(1), 3–8.

Szabo, M. (1994). Enhancing the interactive classroom through computer based instruction: Some examples from P L A T O . In *Computer-mediated communications and the online classroom.* Vol. I. Cresskill, N J : Hampton Press.

Taylor, R. (1980). *The Computer in the school: tutor, tool, tutee.* New York, N Y : Teachers College Press.

Taylor, R. P. (2003). Reflections on the computer in the school. *Contemporary Issues in Technology and Teacher Education,* 3(1). Retrieved from http:// www.citejournal.org/vol3/iss1/seminal/article2.cfm

Texley, J. (1992). Doing without dissection. *The American School Board Journal,* 179(1), 24-26.

Thorburn, D. (2003). Web of paradox. In D. Thorburn & H. Jenkins (Eds.), *Rethinking media change: The aesthetics of transition* (p. 20). Cambridge, M A : M I T Press.

Thorndike, E. L. (1910). The contribution of psychology to education. *The Journal of Educational Psychology*, 1, 5–12.

Thorndike, E. L. (1912). *Education: A first book*. New York, N Y : Macmillan.

Tripathi, A. K. (2002, January). On the Internet: Thinking in action. *Ubiquity*, 42. Retrieved from http://www.acm.org/ubiquity/book _reviews/a_tripathi_2.html

Tuan, Y. F. (2001). *Space and place: The perspective of experience*. Minneapolis, M N : University of Minnesota Press.

Tullis, T. & Albert, W. (2008). *Measuring the user experience: Collecting, analyzing, and presenting usability metrics*. Amsterdam: Elsevier.

Turkle, S. (1984). *The second self: Computers and the human spirit*. New York, N Y : Simon and Schuster.

Turkle, S. (1995). *Life on the screen: Identity in the age of the Internet*. New York, N Y : Simon and Schuster.

Turkle, S. (2005). *The second self: Computers and the human spirit* (20th anniversary ed.). Cambridge, M A : M I T Press.

Usabilityfirst (2010). *Usability glossary*. Retrieved from http://www.usability first.com/glossary/main.cgi

van Manen, M. (1991). *The tact of teaching: The meaning of pedagogical thoughtfulness*. Albany, N Y : State University of New York Press.

van Manen, M. (1997). *Researching lived experience: Human science for an action sensitive pedagogy*, 2nd ed. London, O N : Althouse Press.

van Manen, M. (2002). *Phenomenology online*. Retrieved from http://www .phenomenologyonline.com.

van Manen, M. (2003). *The tone of teaching*. London, O N : Althouse Press.

van Manen, M., & Adams, C. (2009). The phenomenology of space in writing online. *Educational Philosophy and Theory*, 41(1), 10–21.

Waldenfels, B. (2007). *The question of the other* (Tang Chun-I Lecture). Albany, N Y : State University of New York Press.

Wall, M. (2010). *Xbox Indie review: Decay—Part 2. Armless octopus (Blog)*. Retrieved from http://www.armlessoctopus.com/2010/07/15/xbox -indie-review-decay-part-2/

Weaver, G., Green, K., Rahman, A., & Epp, E. (2009). An investigation of online and face-to-face communication in general chemistry. *International Journal for the Scholarship of Teaching and Learning*, 3(1). Retrieved

fromhttp://academics.georgiasouthern.edu/ijsotl/v3n1/articles/PDFs
/Article_WeaverGreenEppRahman.pdf

Weber, S. (1989). Upsetting the set up: Remarks on Heidegger's questing
after technics. *Modern Language Notes*, 104(5), 977–992.

Winograd, D. (2003). The roles, functions and skills of moderators of
online educational computer conferences for distance education. In M.
Corry & C. H. Tu.(Eds.), *Distance education: What works well*. New York,
NY: Haworth Press. Pp. 61-72.

Zembylas, M., & Michaelides, P. (2004). The sound of silence in pedagogy.
*Educational Theory* 54(2), 193–210.

# *Index*

Colin Lankshear & Michele Knobel
*General Editor*s

New literacies and new knowledges are being invented "in the streets" as people from all walks of life wrestle with new technologies, shifting values, changing institutions, and new structures of personality and temperament emerging in a global informational age. These new literacies and ways of knowing remain absent from classrooms. Many educa-tion administrators, teachers, teacher educators, and aca-demics seem largely unaware of them. Others actively oppose them. Yet, they increasingly shape the engagements and worlds of young people in societies like our own. The *New Literacies and Digital Epistemologies* series will ex-plore this terrain with a view to informing educational theory and practice in constructively critical ways.

For further information about the series and submitting manuscripts, please contact:

Michele Knobel & Colin Lankshear
Montclair State University
Dept. of Education and Human Services
3173 University Hall
Montclair, NJ 07043
michele@coatepec.net

To order other books in this series, please contact our Customer Service Department at:

(800) 770-LANG (within the U.S.)
(212) 647-7706 (outside the U.S.)
(212) 647-7707 FAX

Or browse online by series at:

www.peterlang.com